MW00715048

*A'ūdhu billāhi minash-shaitānir-rajīm.*
I seek refuge in God from the accursed satan.

*Bismillāhir-Rahmānir-Rahīm.*
In the name of God,
the Most Compassionate,
the Most Merciful.

# Life
## Is a
# Dream

# Life
## Is a
# Dream
## A Book of Sufi Verse

# M. R. Bawa Muhaiyaddeen

FELLOWSHIP PRESS
Philadelphia, PA

Library of Congress Control Number: 2011933897

Muhaiyaddeen, M. R. Bawa.

Life is a dream: a book of sufi verse/
M. R. Bawa Muhaiyaddeen☻
Philadelphia, PA: Fellowship Press, 2011
p. cm.
includes index.

Trade paperback: 978-0-914390-88-6
Hardcover: 978-0-914390-87-9

1. Sufism.  2. God.  3. Truth.  4. Dream.  5. Reality.  6. Death.
7. Eternal Life.  8. Drama stage of world.  9. Wisdom.  I. Title.

Every attempt is made to ensure the accuracy of the translation of these songs.
They are complete and include the entire content of the songs given by Muhammad
Raheem Bawa Muhaiyaddeen☻ on the dates noted at the beginning of the chapters.

Although the footnotes and glossary have been assembled by the editor and/or translator,
a majority of the explanations and definitions have come directly from
Bawa Muhaiyaddeen's☻ other discourses and songs.

Printed in the United States of America
by FELLOWSHIP PRESS
Bawa Muhaiyaddeen Fellowship
First Printing

MUHAMMAD RAHEEM BAWA MUHAIYADDEEN ◌

# Table of Contents

# Introduction

*A'ūdhu billāhi minash-shaitānir-rajīm.*
*Bismillāhir-Rahmānir-Rahīm.*

As young children in the West, we learned that life is a dream; that nothing lasts and everything changes — the more things change, the more they stay the same. The endless days of the school year were our proof: with rare exceptions, every day was almost exactly like the last and yesterday would surely repeat itself tomorrow. The only way out was to try to fall more deeply asleep or to look out at heaven through the window.

Family life was the same, the job was the same: there was only death at the end of that tunnel. Some of us became intensely aware of the dreaming and of the need to wake up. Many of us went to school some more: like bees who have lost their hive, searching for the way home, taking the same flight path over and over, only to fall senseless from exhaustion. The thought of God began to pervade our hearts.

At that time there were also many gurus and teachers who had come to the United States to set up their wares. Some of us visited their places of business and were momentarily drawn to reach out our hands to pick up what they offered. Certain things were shiny and new, but no guru had what it took to retain us as loyal customers. We went from one guru clone to another, searching, searching, dreaming.

When we finally met Bawa Muhaiyaddeen ☺, he ushered us gently into an entirely new kind of school: the school of grace; he began to share with us a new kind of knowledge: how to distinguish the real from the unreal, the dream from the awakening.

He shared his direct experience with us through every subtle movement of his hands, every flash of light from his eyes; every amazing word came to life. He called us the jeweled lights of his eyes and something happened. The foxes and the crocodiles from the fables he told us were there in the room with us. When he shared his experiences they became real, they pervaded the school-room.

The moment we stepped into his room we were in a different universe, a universe that was awake, that moved, that spoke, that was alive. We came back to that school-room, day after day, never knowing who we would find there: angels, saints, prophets, Adam or Noah, Abraham or Ishmael, Moses or David, Jesus or Muhammad, may the peace of God be upon them all.

We soon had proof of what we had already begun to imagine: the only way out of the dream was to directly experience oneness with God. He let us perceive what that experience was like. The transmission of those blissful experiences was vivid in the songs he sang, the thousands and thousands of spontaneous songs about the nature of God and the nature of the dream that was our life in the world.

It is the sound of these songs that brings to us the experience of God as the only reality; the sound is both unique and exquisitely familiar: no sounds in this world even come close, yet we know we know them from a time before memory began.

There are only a few of those thousands of songs in this book and they have been translated into English from the Tamil only by the grace of God. The reason they are in book form is to preserve the words: Bawangal ☺ told us that in the future, only the books would survive. May God bestow upon us the *īmān* and the love to always be attuned to these teachings, may we experience them as God intends.

Following are Bawa Muhaiyaddeen's own words from a talk he gave on September 1, 1979, describing how he learned:

> "I am a student; I am learning. My work has been to learn from all the prophets and the *rasūls,* messengers of Allāh. I am a student who is learning. As I learned, I studied some of their stories somewhat well. I learned with understanding. Because I learned as a student, I did not see them as having died. I did not see them as gone. They were the ones who had to teach me and I was the one who had to learn.

> "Because they had to teach me, they had not changed. They teach me. They are alive. They have taught me their *wilāyāt*[1] and the duties they do, the service they do. I have learned through my eyes, my *qalb,* heart, and my wisdom from them; it is because I am a student that I see them. This is one section out of the many sections I have understood. These are the *sayyids,*[2] the shaikhs, and *rasūls* from whom I have learned.

> "Now and forever, they are my shaikhs. I did not study in a school. I did not study in Arabic. I do not know Arabic.

---

1. *wilāyāt* (Arabic n.) the names and actions of God
2. *sayyids* (Arabic n.) a title of respect used for a descendant of Prophet Muhammad ☻; lords, leaders, chieftains

I did not study in Tamil, either. Nor do I know English; I do not know any language very well. I did not study in school, and I do not know these languages; I have not learned them. It is from these *rasūls* and *sayyids* that I have studied. According to my experience, they are alive.

"If you can become students, you can learn from them. However, if you learn this knowledge, the *dunyā,* the world, will not accept you. Why? What the *dunyā* studies is different from the teachings of the prophets. The religions will not accept you. Why? The teachings of the prophets are: your life is all lives; everyone's sorrow is your sorrow; everyone's illness is your illness; everyone's happiness is your happiness—there is so much, it cannot be described. Their form is absolute compassion. Their life is absolute truth. The certitude of *īmān* is their seed, the seed of wisdom. Their wisdom is absolute resplendence. The Light of God grows from that wisdom.

"As we study this state, as we learn in this state, the world and the earth itself will oppose us. Wealth will oppose us. Land will oppose us. Woman will oppose us. Shaitān will despise us. All the evil qualities will oppose us. Maya will oppose us. Arrogance will oppose us. That which is the 'I' will oppose us. The religions, the religions of separation will oppose us.

"Titles will oppose us. Egotism will oppose us. Jealousy will oppose us. Selfishness will oppose us. Blood ties will oppose us. Color, 'my ethnic group/your ethnic group, my color' will oppose us. 'My scripture/your scripture' will oppose us. 'My religion/your religion' will oppose us. 'My philosophy/your philosophy' will oppose us. 'I am different/you are different' will oppose us. These and similar things will all oppose us. They will drive us away. They will drive us away, 'Get out! Get out!' These are their teachings.

"They will drive us away just as they drove the prophets away. They will drive us away just as they drove the *rasūls* away. They will come to kill us just as they came to kill them. They will come to imprison us just as they came to imprison them. They will torture us just as they tortured them. We will be homeless just as they were homeless. We will not have clothes to wear just as they did not have clothes to wear. The world will hurt us, ridicule us, drive us away, and banish us in the same way.

"Their knowledge was obtained in that state. If we study this knowledge, it will not come from a book. It will come directly, as God's words. They must tell us God's words directly. The meaning of those words is alive. That state is the state in which we must learn; we must become students in that state.

"If those who become shaikhs or gurus, great in religion, great in their ethnic group, great in wealth, spiritual, or great in school, assume these titles, they will not learn. They will never learn.

"We must remain students, dedicating ourselves to our Shaikh, dedicating our bodies, our belongings, and our lives to Him, giving Him the responsibility; then, if we bow in obeisance before Him, we will learn. May we think of this. There are many fundamental things like this, and if we think about them, we will understand. It is like this.

"But the others, those who say 'I', those who call themselves gurus have already died and are going to hell. They are the demons here; they are the ones we see here.

"Instead, we must see those who have the open hearts, the open *qalbs*. It is the prophets who are alive. They are the ones we must learn from. We cannot learn from the dead. We must understand with wisdom. If we know, we can understand and learn truth. This is the truth. I am still learning, through experience: I ask you things and I learn; I ask them, they tell me, and I learn with understanding. This is my school.

"If each child would think of this and teach their children about the True Ones, telling them, 'Try to learn from those who were not born and who will not die; become a student,' you will succeed.

"Do you understand, my child?

"All right, precious children, jeweled lights of my eyes, I have to feed you. I have to give you food; I have to make a curry now."

May God grant us the grace to also learn in this way. May we learn what we came here to learn.

-Crisi (Muhammad Muhaiyaddeen Fatima)

# Life
## Is a
# Dream

# I Had a Dream

*from Gnāna Oli Malay, Prayer Beads of
the Light of Divine Knowledge*

*c. 1946*

I HAD A DREAM, I had a dream,
about casting off my cares,
closing my eyes,
and sleeping without sleeping,

about driving out the horrible monkey,
mounting the horse of the breath,[1] and riding away.

I had a dream, I had a dream,
about casting off my cares,
closing my eyes,
and sleeping without sleeping,

about slipping gently into the green-color,
about two becoming indivisibly One.

I had a dream, I had a dream,
about casting off my cares,
closing my eyes,
and sleeping without sleeping,

---

1. horse of the breath: the *dhikr, lā ilāha illAllāhu*

about beating off and banishing the five entities,
and dwelling with the Blissful Guru
in a state of true love.

I had a dream, I had a dream,
about casting off my cares,
closing my eyes,
and sleeping without sleeping,

about journeying and arriving in Chennai,[2]
meeting and embracing the
King of the City of Chennai.

I had a dream, I had a dream,
about casting off my cares,
closing my eyes,
and sleeping without sleeping,

about climbing the rungs of the ladder, ascending,
embracing and holding on to my Highest One.

I had a dream, I had a dream,
about casting off my cares,
closing my eyes,
and sleeping without sleeping,

about humbly walking towards my Bridegroom,
the wedding necklace fastened around my neck.

---

2. Chennai (n.) [Lit. the city of Chennai in India, formerly Madras] Chennai
symbolizes the liberation that results from annihilation of the self.

I had a dream, I had a dream,
about casting off my cares,
closing my eyes,
and sleeping without sleeping,

about living with purity and happiness,
holding the rudder firmly and steering with ease.

I had a dream, I had a dream,
about casting off my cares,
closing my eyes,
and sleeping without sleeping,

about setting the mast,
boarding the ship and sailing away.

I had a dream, I had a dream,
about casting off my cares,
closing my eyes,
and sleeping without sleeping,

about finding and dispelling that
which appeared and was born with me,
and establishing the Silent Potter there in its place.

I had a dream, I had a dream,
about casting off my cares,
closing my eyes,
and sleeping without sleeping,

about truly knowing the five and the six,
gazing at my Father and boarding the ship.

I had a dream, I had a dream,
about casting off my cares,
closing my eyes,
and sleeping without sleeping,

about pushing aside the honors, learning my lessons,
and acknowledging the beggar requesting alms.

I had a dream, I had a dream,
about casting off my cares,
closing my eyes,
and sleeping without sleeping,

about holding the arm of my own Bridegroom.
The two of us are happy together, yet I give my self away.

I had a dream, I had a dream,
about casting off my cares,
closing my eyes,
and sleeping without sleeping,

about regarding my Bridegroom
with overwhelming joy,
mounting the King's elephant of grace and flying away.

I had a dream, I had a dream,
about casting off my cares,
closing my eyes,
and sleeping without sleeping.

# Melting with Love

MELTING WITH LOVE, melting with love,
O God, jeweled Light of the eye of *gnānam*,[1]
O God, jeweled Light of the eye of *gnānam*,
our *qalbs* are melting with love,
melting with grace.
The *qalb*, the heart of the heart,
is melting at the sight of
Your overflowing beauty,
Your melting beauty.

O jeweled Light of the eye of grace,
come to us.
Grant us Your grace, protect us.
Give us Your love and Your qualities of grace.
May that grace come from our *qalbs,* our *qalbs,*
like fragrance comes from flowers,
like fragrance comes from flowers.

Protect us, watch over us, grant us Your grace,
O my Eye, O my God, O Qādir.

---

1. *gnānam* (n.) divine wisdom, grace-awakened wisdom, divine knowledge

You are the most exalted Crown Jewel
of the lives in the earth and of the lives in the sky.
You are inside and outside, and
You are the One who rules them from within.

You are the One who is in our eyes and in our *qalbs,*
as the pupil.
Grant us the meaning with Your grace.
Rule over us, my Almighty One.
Come from the skies and from the earth
as the Transcendent One.

You are God who is commingled
with the light of the eyes, in the center.
Come as the honey, as the jewel of the *qalb.*
O ripe fruit of the Compassion within my love,
grant us Your grace.
Grant us Your grace from inside
the heart of love within all lives.

O Master of All Things,
You must come into their hearts
and protect them from within.
Help them and grant them Your blessing,
from the skies and from the earth.
Give them the eye of the Light of *gnānam*
in the forehead, between the [physical] eyes.

You must dwell in our *qalbs,* and
grant us Your grace from there.

O our God, jeweled Light of our eyes,
please come to us.
God of love,
tranquil jeweled Light of the eye,
You must come to us.
You must grant Your grace
from within the hearts of all my beloved ones
who have been born with me.

The world of the earth and
the world of the sky are our worlds.
Your world is within them.
You are the One who belongs to us.
Please come to us.

O our Gem,
O our Eye for the Day of Resurrection,
beloved One, O God,
please come to us and grant us Your grace.
You are our Creator, the One who made us.
O God, please come to us and grant us Your grace.

You are within the five.
You are within the heart.
You must grant us Your grace without delay.
You are within the *qalb,*
as the jeweled Light of its eye, in its center.
You must help us and grant us Your grace from within.

You must grant us Your grace and correct
this incorrigible heart.
You must grant us Your grace so that
this unclear heart can praise You.
O God, You must come to give us Your grace.
O Gem of grace,
O Gem of grace,
You must come to give us Your grace.

O Divine One, jeweled Light of the eye of *gnānam,*
O my God,
You are the One who is the object of our meditation.
You are the Eternal Father of *gnānam.*

You must end the suffering of Your servants.
You must grant us the grace that is within Your love.
In the *qalb* You are the Creator who is God.
Please grant us the blessing of Your grace.

You must come to cut away
our sins, evil deeds, and anger
with Your grace.
You must bless us with
the truth, Your grace, and Your qualities,
my Father, O God.

You must open our hearts,
come to grant us Your grace, and correct
the five, the five elements
that rule within the *qalb,*
O our God.

You are the Light of the Gem,
our Jewel, the jeweled Light of the eye of the *qalb*
for the Day of Resurrection,
O our Father of wisdom, our God.
Give us Your love.
Come, grant us Your grace.
Protect us, we who are the poor ones.
Dispel the evil that is known as hell.
Dispel the darkness that is known as sin.
Give us the Light that is known as truth.
Correct our hearts with Your grace.

Then, now, and forever,
You are our God who gives us grace.
O Light of the eye of *gnānam,*
come to us.
Turn us towards goodness with certainty.
We need Your blessing
so that the praise that comes from our *qalbs,*
from our hearts,
emerges like fragrance does from flowers.
You must comfort all these loving hearts.

Medicine of grace, O our God,
we need Your grace.
You must dispel all the
arrogance, anger, and sin
that exist in these six ways in the heart.
Rule over us and grant us Your qualities with grace.

Grant us Your tolerance and peace with love.
Grant us justice, integrity, good conscience,
good conduct, and the ability to pray to You,
O Almighty One,
O Rahmān, O Most Merciful One.
O Possessor of the eye of compassion,
give us the wealth of compassion, O God.
We do not know the five within us.
You are the Knower who recites with wisdom.
You are the Father, You are the form of bliss.
You are the eternal Treasure of both our worlds, O God.

You must remain in our hearts.
Help us with Your grace.
Give us the Light of *gnānam*.
Give us the good state.
Give us Your grace.
O Most Perfect One,
You must stay within, and
grant Your grace from inside
the hearts of those who have been born with me.

Omnipresent One, O Rahmān, O Most Merciful One,
dispel the wrongs we have committed.
Correct this incorrigible heart.
Grant us Your wondrous qualities,
Your unique beauty,
the blessing of Your compassion, and
the completion of Your beauty
that is the wealth of grace.

Come as a wondrous blessing.
Grant us Your grace.
O Most Gracious One,
O Rahmān, O Most Merciful One,
grant us Your grace.
You must remain in the hearts of
all who have been born with me,
and grant them Your grace
so that they do not experience
sadness, poverty, or illness.
You must grant them Your grace
so that poverty, illness, and disease
do not touch them.

You must cut away the illnesses of their minds
with Your peace.
You must give them the ever-living herb of grace,
with Your grace, O Almighty One.
You must grant that grace inside all their hearts.
You must be the Truth within truth there and help them.

O Perfect One, O Rahmān, O Most Merciful One,
Eternal One,
Pādishah of both worlds,
O my Father,
O my Father,
yā Rabbal-'ālamīn, O Creator of All the Universes.
*Āmīn. Āmīn.*

Come, grant us Your grace.
Come, grant us Your grace.
Come, grant us Your grace.

*Āmīn. Āmīn.* May it be so. May it be so.
Yā Rabbal-ʿālamīn, O Creator of All the Universes,
protect us and give us Your grace.

# Time to Wake Up

*c. 1974*

O*Y MANAMĒ,*[1] O walking corpse,
believe, believe, believe that
what the world has divided is all false,
what the world has looked at is false.

Race, religion, separation, time, the hours,
the designated times, all of it—
God has none of it,
wisdom has none of it,
the truth and His grace have none of it.

Prayer, *toluhay,* and *'ibādah*[2] all belong to God.
Prayer, *toluhay,* and *'ibādah* all belong to God.
Look.
They have no time, no hour, no season,
no great day, no small day.
There is no time for Him.

---

1. *manamē* (n.) heart, mind, self, life

2. *toluhay* (n.) worship, prayer; most often refers to the formal five-times prayer in Islām; *'ibādah* (Arabic n.) worship and service to God

He is always the One without a season,
the One without time,
the One without end,
the One without day,
the One without beginning and end,
the One without a start and a finish,
the One without birth and death,
the One without parents and ancestors,
the One without a good day and a bad day,
the One without time and season,
the One without a clock and an hour.

What bad day or good day could He have?
Realize this, O mind.
For Him and for worship and prayer to Him,
what time is there?
What hour is there?
He is always intermingled in your body and your life;
that is His beginningless and endless day.
Time. Hours. Minutes.
He does not have them. Look.
That is how to worship Him, look carefully.

*Oy,* Baby Mother,[3]
*oy,* Myrna pillay,[4]
*aye,* Crisi pillay,

---

3. Bawangal ☺ often sang directly to whoever was in his presence, incorporating the children and the surroundings into a song calling us—and all of you—to God.
4. pillay (n.) child

*ee,* Jeanne pillay,
*ooh,* June pillay,
*ooh,* June pillay.
All of you, recite and pray like this;
place your intention upon Him and search for Him, come.

Gather around Him,
intend to pray to the One
who has no time, no minutes, no season,
no beginning, no end.
He is the One who does not even have one second.
He is the One who has no time.
You must always pray.
Every second, every moment,
every minute you must worship Him.

Man has divided the seasons.
He has determined the days and the nights and
when they begin and end.
Seven days:
Sunday, Sunday, Monday, Tuesday, Wednesday,
Friday, Saturday, Sunday,
Saturday, Saturday, Tuesday, Saturday, Sunday,
Monday and days like this.
Like the days of the week, man has set the races
and religions in many ways.
Man has set the time and the prayers.
The times: the good days, the bad days, all the days,
that day and this day are business days.

He has none of that.
The only day is God's day.
All time is made of His minutes.
All time is His day.
He is Time.
He is God.
He is Time.
He is the Creator.
He is the One who prays.
He is the One who accepts the prayer.
He is the One who watches.
He is the One who asks the questions.
He is the One who gives the judgment.
Try to know Him. You!

*Oy!* The storm and the wind are coming.
The rain is coming.
Friday is coming. Pray day is coming.
Early this morning those who left for Yālpanam,[5]
those who left for Yālpanam are now on the train;
those who left for work are on their way to work;
those who are sleeping are lying down.
Gnaniyar and Arabi are lying down and sleeping.
Kāmil tambi,[6] Rick, Stan, Teacher pillay,
pillay and I, and Tavvam are sitting up.
We are here.

---

5. Yālpanam (n.) Jaffna, a city in northern Sri Lanka
6. tambi (n.) brother

Two or three are lying down.
Baby Mother and June,
Baby Mother and June.
*Ah!*
Baby Mother and June
and Crisi pillay are sitting up.
The three lazy ones are lying down —
four of them!
They are lazily sleeping,
lazily sleeping.
This is how all of us are here.

*Ay!*
The crows are singing, the birds are dancing.
The rain is falling, the lightning is coming.
The wind is coming, the storm is coming.
The trees are dancing.
The time and the minutes are here.
All the birds are calling.
*Ay!* They are all calling.
Calling, screeching, shouting.
The birds are all calling, screeching, shouting.

This is the world.
It is time for everyone to get up.
This is the world.
This is the time and the minute to pray to God.
See God and pray to Him every day at all times
and in all minutes.

*Oy,* Baby Mother, Āmi Mother, Swami Mother. *Oy!*
Go drink tea.
Wash your faces.
Go to the bathroom.
Drink tea.
Come back!

Right.
There is a cold in my nose.
Arabi rāni[7] is on the left.
English rāni is on the right.
We are all in the middle.
We are all in the middle.
The storm and the rain and the wind are in the world.
The storm and the rain and the wind are all around
in the circle of the world,
in the circle of the world.
We are all in the middle.

*Ay!*
Arabi rāni is on the left.
English rāni is on the right.
We are in the middle, and
the storm, the rain, and the wind are all around.
All around, all around.

---

7. rāni (n.) Queen. Just as a parent would, Bawangal ☺ used certain nicknames for us.

*Ay!*
Baby Mother, Kāmil tambi, Jean, Ann are in the middle.
Arabi rāni is on the left.
English rāni is on the right.
We are in the middle, and
the storm, the rain, and the wind are all around.
All around, all around.
Baby Mother, Kāmil tambi, Jean.
The Arab country rāni is on the left.
The English rāni is on the right.
The storm, the rain, and the wind are all around.
All around, all around.

*Ay! Hmm.*
This is the world.
That is the world.
Look at how the birds and winged creatures are calling.
Listen to how they are screeching in the rain and the wind.

*Kee kee kee.*
The storm, the rain, and the wind are all around.
The birds are calling *keekeekeekee, kaakaakaakaa,
kookookookoo.*
They are all screeching in the rain,
*keekeekeekee, kookookookoo.*

You must protect us with Your grace.
This is the world.
There is rain here.
There are storms here.

There is wind here.
There is sunshine here.
There is sadness here.
There is happiness here.

There are blood ties, husbands, children —
all of them are here.
The earth, the sky, and the body are here.
The sun, the moon, the stars, and the night are here.
Night and day are here.
We are in the middle.
You are in the middle of that.

*Ay!*
We are in the middle.
All of creation is here.
And You are in the middle of creation,
O God, You are in the middle of it.
You have no darkness,
no sadness, no night, no day,
no time at all, no hour, no season,
no storm, no rain, no wind.

O God, jeweled Light of my eye,
You have no time, no season, no sadness, no difficulty,
no ties, no attachment at all.
You have no illness, no disease, no poverty, no hunger,
no wife, no child, no puppies, no livestock, no cattle.
You have none of them.

You have no happiness, no sadness at all,
no night, no day, no birth, no death.
You are the One who gave us
the seasons, the hours, the time, the birth, and the death.
The night and the day, the sun and the moon,
the time, the hours and the minutes,
the storms, the wind, the sun,
You put them here.
You made it creation.
And You destined us to be here.

The world is all around us.
The air is around the world.
The water is around the air.
The storms are around the water.
The storms are around the water, the water.
Many, many, many, many kinds of rain and colors are
around the storms
and the thunder and lightning.
The thunder is all around,
and we are in the middle.
Sadness, happiness, sorrow, difficulty,
hunger, illness, old age, death.
With this body are the five elements, and
from them we get constant trouble.

We are caught in the maya and darkness
and the pain caused by the mind and the blood ties,
the blood ties of maya.

The daughters, the husband, the wife, the mother,
the father, all of us
get together and cry, *"aiy yai yo!"*
We cry-*yooo.*
"Child, mother, father, child, wife, knife, *aiyooo!"*
we shout.

End this sorrow.
You have none of it.
You are in the middle!
The world is all around us.

# Allāh Is Sufficient for Our *Qalbs*

*c. 1974*

HAVE *TAWAKKUL*, surrender to God, every second. Say, *"Al-hamdu lillāh*, all praise is to God," every second. That is success. If you know the truth, you will have no misfortune.

*[Bawangal ☺ begins to sing:]*

> If you know the truth,
> you will have no misfortune.
>
> If you know yourself,
> you will know your Master.
>
> If you know the earth,
> you will know the meaning of silence.
>
> If you abandon your own comfort,
> you will know the comfort of others.
> You will know the completion of life in this world.
> You will know the meaning of your life in this world.
>
> If you realize yourself,
> the world will shrink.

If your wisdom grows,
the Light of grace will rise.

If you abandon your physical perceptions,
compassion will come to fill you.

If you abandon the visions seen by your eyes,
the Light of God's compassion will
come to complete you.

If you know the earth,
you will know the sore that is the mind.

If you abandon your self,
you will become your Master.

If you know your life,
you will know the Light of truth.

If you know all of this,
you will not exist;
you will not stay here.

If you open your eyes,
you will understand the compassion
of the lives in the world.
The path to reach peace will be open.
You will know the peaceful state of the world,
and you will praise it.

You will say, *"Al-hamd,"*[1] and praise Him.
You will say, *"Tawakkul-'alAllāh,"*[2]
about everything that is happening,
and you will have peace.
You will live without the duality
of happiness or sadness.

The eight-span body
will become a golden Light.
The body of *insān,* of man,
will become a golden Light.
Grace will join with the Light, and
it will shine there.
Bliss! Bliss! You will see nothing
other than God.

Without separation,
without race,
without bile,
without darkness,
without connection to sadness or happiness,
freedom will be yours, and
you will know the life that belongs to you.
Your heart will know what happiness is.

It will know everything, and
the grace of God will dawn.

---

1. *al-hamd, al-hamdu lillāh* (Arabic) all praise is to God
2. *tawakkul-'alAllāh* (Arabic) surrender to God; to hand over all responsibilities to God

That which was born on the earth and
from maya will perish.
Arrogance, karma, and maya will perish—
not even their roots will remain.
Desire for earth, desire for woman, desire for gold
will leave you.

The silence, the breath, and God will remain.
To be in this state
is to become the words of God.
His words will be in your breath and in your words.
His vision will be in your eyes,
in the pupils of your eyes.
His sound will be in your ears.

When all other explanations are annihilated,
His fundamental Truth will be One.
It is in this state that success will exist for you.
When everything is God,
that will be sufficient.
It is then that the word, "Enough!" will be born.

All the evil actions will leave by themselves.
All the destruction will be dispelled.
Everything other than God will become nonexistent.
Your possession and your belonging will be the One.
He will become your Helpmate and your Grace.
He will be in the earth, in the sky, and everywhere.
He will be intermingled
in your heart, in your life, in the Light.

He will dawn resonantly
from the wisdom as Light.
The life in which
He is the only One who exists
is exalted.

Then you will see your duty to all lives.
You will become a slave to all of those lives.
You will help those lives.
You will dispel the sadness in all those lives.
They will reach happiness, and
their hearts will open.

All lives will see the compassion there.
When your own need for comfort leaves you,
when the comfort of others becomes your comfort,
when that occurs,
the heart will become Light.

On that shining day,
everything in your life will be laid open.
If you know the heart,
light will dawn in your face.
If your heart is clear,
you will understand Ādi.[3]
This state will become the color of Light.

The heart will become resonant, and
the kingdom of God will become luminous there.

---

3. Ādi (n.) God

Nothing other than God
will exist in this world.
Other than His actions,
what happiness will you have in your life?

Then there will be no good people or bad people
for you in this world.
Your existence will be comprised of only good people.
Then ignorance and lack of wisdom will cease to exist.
Then your bliss will become love for all lives.
When you attain this state,
you will become God.
That state will be the exaltedness of your life.
Then you will be a messenger of God.
You will be a messenger of God,
and God's grace will be yours.

When those two become one,
that is life.
When the exaltedness and the Light of life
exist in that state,
you will be Man and God.
That will become the Light of *insān kāmil,* perfected Man.
That will become luminous
and dawn in the world as the Qutb ☺.4

---

4. Qutb ☺ (Arabic n.) One who has attained the power of the Light of grace-awakened divine analytic wisdom that dawned from the throne of God and that investigates, understands, and analyzes everything in the eighteen thousand universes and beyond; through this inner analysis, the darkness of evil is dispelled and the beauty of goodness is made clear and radiant. Sent by Allāh, through His grace and mercy, to reawaken mankind's faith in God and to establish certitude in our hearts, the Qutb ☺ is the wondrous embodiment and illustration of *īmān,* absolute faith in God, in all three worlds.

When that fills the heart,
it becomes Ahamad.[5]
When the face blooms with beauty,
it becomes Muhammad.
When the completion of wisdom is attained,
it shines as the Light of Nūr Muhammad.[6]
Then the two that were Allāhu and Muhammad
become One.
Then you will attain the state
in which you exist as Him.
Realize and look at this state.

Give everything into His responsibility.
When you praise only Him,
the happiness of that will make your life complete.
Then that completion will be enough.
Then patience, tolerance, and the state of peace
will be the birthright of your life.
The *sabūr, shukūr, tawakkul, al-hamdu,*[7] and peace
will be the Light in our *qalbs,* our inner hearts.
That will become the state
of meditation, prayer, and worship.
That will come to you, embrace you,
and complete you.

---

5. Ahamad (Arabic & Tamil n.) the beauty of the heart. [Lit. *aham* (n.) heart; *muham* (n.) face]

6. Nūr Muhammad (Arabic n.) one of the nine aspects of Muhammad, the aspect that is wisdom

7. *sabūr, shukūr, tawakkul,* and *al-hamdu* (Arabic n.) inner patience, contentment, surrender to God, and all praise to God

Then when you praise Him and say, "Enough!"
Allāh will come to you
as the Meaning and as the Grace.
He will be the Meaning and the Grace within you.
He will be the exaltedness of your life
and the Light within you.
The completion and the duty will be within you.
You will attain a life of peace and tranquility.

Realize this state with wisdom.
Open your heart and look into the wisdom.
Cut off the mind,
be clear with wisdom.
The Grace will be luminous within the exaltedness there.
If you come to cherish the Grace and pray,
you will attain peace in this world.

*Al-hamdu lillāh,* all praise is to God. You must think of this and look into it. What are you doing? What are your actions? You must act with wisdom. Enough. *Al-hamdu lillāh. Tawakkulun 'alAllāh.* Enough. What we get is enough. If He gives us gold, that is enough. If He gives us earth, that is enough. If He gives us buriyani, that is enough, *al-hamdu lillāh.* If He gives us water, *al-hamdu lillāh.* Whatever we get at the time, at the *waqt,*[8] *al-hamdu lillāh.* You must think of this.

If you do not accept this, there will come a time when nothing will remain with you. *Tangom*[9]—we will go. *Selvom*[10]—we

---

8. *waqt* (Arabic n.) commonly refers to the duration of time ordained during which the five daily prayers can be performed.
9. *tangom* (phrase) we will go; *tangam* (n.) gold
10. *selvom* (phrase) we will leave; *selvam* (n.) wealth

will leave. *Tarittirom*[11]—we will not tarry. You must somehow manage with what you have and try to live in an appropriate way. You might have to live here or there. You must accept whatever comes at the time.

When this *waqt* is over—*al-hamdu lillāh*. You must not think of the next *waqt*. *Tawakkulun 'alAllāh*. You must say *al-hamdu lillāh* at every *waqt*. You must say *al-hamdu lillāh* for what is to come in the next *waqt*. You must have *shukūr*, contentment, for what comes in this *waqt*. *Al-hamdu lillāh*, have *shukūr*. For what is to come in the next *waqt*—*tawakkulun 'alAllāh*. Have *sabūr*, inner patience. Spend your time in this way. Then the next *waqt* and the next will also pass. If you say this during every *waqt*...

Say *tawakkulun 'alAllāh* for what is to come in the next *waqt*. Have *sabūr*. *Tawakkulun 'alAllāh*. Then each second will pass in this way and sorrow will not come to you.

Sadness will not come to you. Unhappiness will not come to you. Say it at this *waqt*. Then it will be over. Say it at the next *waqt*. Then that will be over. The *waqt* after that—*tawakkul, al-hamdu lillāh*. Do this continuously for everything that comes. Then you will have peace and tranquility. Then nothing will bother you; nothing will destroy you. You will not be destroyed. If each of you can attain this state, that will be good. *Al-hamdu lillāh*. You must think of this. *Shari*, all right.

God's patience, God's tolerance. You must give room to others. You must give your happiness to others. When you accept the sorrows of others, you will be God. Thank you.

---

11. *tarittirom* (phrase) we will not tarry; *tarittiram* (n.) troubles

# Those Whose
# Good Hearts Melt

*c. 1974*

THOSE WHOSE GOOD hearts melt
will find the blessing they seek.
Those whose good hearts melt
will find the blessing they seek.

God will contemplate and melt into the world
within the heart that melts and dissolves,
within the heart that melts and dissolves.
The love that contemplates God will melt
in the *qalb* of the heart that melts and dissolves,
in the heart that melts —
look, His grace will melt in your *qalb*,
your inner heart.

When determination begins to emerge in you,
strength of faith and His *rahmah*, His grace,
will flow from your *qalb* like honey.
When you believe in the Almighty One,
He will believe in you and
serve you all the days of your life.

When happiness and faith come into your heart,
the unfathomable Ruler of Grace
will focus His incomparable love upon you.
Day and night He will make grace and wisdom
resonate in the love within your heart.

When you see the shore of your heart,
He will give to your *qalb*
His kingdom and the path of His justice,
as His treasure in trust.

When your desire and attachment,
your trust and love have settled upon Him,
He will give to you
the entire birthright of your life,
His exaltedness and His wealth, and
He will dwell with you forever.

He is Truth without falsehood,
He is the One who is Truth.
The Good One who does not backbite,
the Father without anger,
the Almighty One who is compassionate justice—
if you always believe in Him,
your heart itself will become your wealth.

He will melt into love.
Your entire heart will become pure.
In truth, your heart will become the heaven that is paradise.
Then, without leaving you for even a day,

He will never withdraw from you.
He will remain with you.
He will always serve you,
the One who bears the name God.

Beloved jeweled lights of my eyes,
children of grace and wisdom,
establish your certitude and determination in Him.
Contemplate and have certitude.
Rely on Him with determination,
cling to Him with wisdom.
Then you can always succeed.
Then this worldly life will become heaven for you.

He is the One who does the duty that is good
to those who are good and to everyone.
If you do His duty
with all your thoughts and intentions,
you can have contentment, peace, and
tranquility in this world.

You are my eyes and the lights within them.
You are the jeweled lights that fill my eyes.
Children, beloved to my *qalb,*
search for the treasured qualities.
Act with the actions that God gave to you
as your birthright.

With faith and trust,
search for Him each day and night.

If you search for Him
with your breath and with your words,
just as light exists in the center of the pupil of your eye,
He will be the Light of day within your *qalb*.
If you search for that within yourself,
He will be the Light of day within your *qalb*.
Then you can reach salvation.
Then you can reach exaltedness in your life in the world,
and you can obtain eternal success.

Jeweled lights of my eyes,
do God's duty in your hearts.
With boundless, melting hearts,
search for the boundless assistance of He who is One.

If you keep Him in your hearts day and night,
He will remain there,
becoming the expanding ray of Light.
That will change destinies.
Karma will be dispelled,
and the kingdom of God, who is our Creator,
will become complete in your *qalb*.

The kingdom of the three worlds,
life in the three worlds,
the treasures of the *mubārakāt*,
the blessings of the three worlds,
will become your birthright.
He will make them yours in completion,
in your life in this world.

If you think with wisdom,
certitude, determination, and *īmān*,
if you believe with certitude,
He will never leave you in this world.
He will remain resonating in your heart,
serving all lives.
Day and night,
He will stay in the hearts of good people.

Loving children,
jeweled lights who have received the grace of God,
search for the melting love
with awareness and wisdom;
make the intention to do His duty.

Then He will always bless you.
He will heal all your illnesses.
Even if your mother and father forget you,
He will always do His duty,
and never forget you.
No evil will ever harm you.
Your heart will become heaven.
The Light of grace will be there.
Your heart will become heaven.
God will rule from within it.

Then this world and the next world will be overcome.
He will give you life without death.
He will give you the wealth to not be reborn,
the wealth of grace.
Then you can live in this world,
free of this world and the next.

You must comfort my children
who are the jeweled lights of my eyes.
May Your Heart become their birthright.
Please melt their hearts with Your truth.

Focus on the One who does only what is good.
Place your intention upon Him at all times.
Search for Him in your *qalb*.
Think of Him with wisdom.
Make Him dissolve into your awareness.
Merge with Him through your actions.
Do your duties.
Do your duties in the three worlds.
Help all lives.
Live doing your duty,
  showing peace, tranquility, and serenity to everyone.
Live in order to do duty,
  then your Creator will help you in this world.

In order to receive your Father's grace,
you need Allāh's love, grace, and wisdom.
You need faith and certitude.
You need determination and prayer.
Melt your *qalb* so you can do duty with good conduct.
If you melt like candle wax,
He will intermingle with you as Light.
*Āmīn. Āmīn*, yā Rabbal-'ālamīn.
May it be so. May it be so,
O Creator of All the Universes.

# Allāhu, Allāh

*Monday, June 24, 1974, 7:00 P.M.*

Aʟʟᴀ̄ʜᴜ, Aʟʟᴀ̄ʜ,
Allāhu, Allāh, One without anyone else, Allāh.
Allāhu, Allāh, One without anyone else, our Allāh,
our One without anyone else, Allāh.
The Complete One, Allāh.
The Complete One, Allāh.
O Eternal One, Allāh.
Allāhu, Allāh, One without anyone else, Allāh.

You are the One who is the Sound and the Resonance,
Allāh.
You are the One who dwells alone and rules, Allāh.
Allāhu, Allāh, One without anyone else, Allāh.
You are the One who is filled with compassion, Allāh.
You are the One who dwells in all visible things, Allāh.
Allāhu, Allāh, the One who rules without anyone else,
our Allāh.

Existing without deviating from the path of justice,
ruling everywhere eternally,
existing everywhere, omnipresent, as the source of all things,
the One who knows the *qalb* and grants assistance, Allāh.

Allāhu, Allāh, One without anyone else, Allāh.
Helper to the helper, Allāh.
The One who helps all the messengers, Allāh.
The One who gives the commandments, Allāh.
The One who bestows the protection of
compassionate love, Allāh.
Allāhu, Allāh, One without anyone else, Allāh.
You are One without anyone else, Allāh.

You are the One who fills the heart within the heart, Allāh.
You grant Your grace to the three worlds, Allāh.
You are the Protector who will go
on the path of justice, Allāh.
You are the One who is always omnipresent, Allāh.
Allāhu, Allāh, One without anyone else, Allāh.
Allāhu, Allāh, One without anyone else, Allāh,
One without anyone else, Allāh.

You are the Pure One without beginning or end, Allāh.
You are the Pure One without beginning or end, Allāh.
You are the Creator of the messengers and prophets, Allāh.
You are the One who teaches
through the commandments, Allāh.
You are the One who sent down all
Your commandments with grace, Allāh.
Allāhu, Allāh, One without anyone else, Allāh.
You are One without anyone else, Allāh.
You are One without anyone else, Allāh.

You are intermingled as *Qalb* within *qalb,* Allāh.
You are the Dispeller of all karma, Allāh.
You are the One who dwells within goodness, Allāh.
You are the One who knows everything in the land, Allāh.
Allāhu, Allāh, Allāhu, Allāh,
One without anyone else, Allāh.
He is One without anyone else, Allāh.

He is the One who is there in birth and in death, Allāh.
He is the One who treats everyone equally, Allāh.
He is the One who sees with the eye of compassion, Allāh.
He is the One who heals the
inherited karmic illnesses, Allāh.
Allāhu, Allāh, One without anyone else, You are Allāh.

He is One without wife, children, or birth, Allāh.
He is One without bile or obsession, Allāh.
He is the One who exists without anything else, Allāh.
He has no this world or next world,
He is the Eternal One, Allāh.
Allāhu, Allāh, One without anyone else, You are Allāh.
Allāhu, Allāh, the Treasure without anyone else,
You alone are Allāh.

The One who knows the beginning and the end
of prayers, worship, and *'ibādah,* Allāh.
Understanding *'ibādah, dhikr,* and *fikr,*
service to God, remembrance of God, and
contemplation of God,

41

knowing their beginning and the end inside the heart,
He is the Almighty One who grants
the success that lasts forever.
IllAllāhu, O God, You are Allāh.
Allāhu, Allāh, One without anyone else,
You alone are Allāh.


The One without parallel or help, Allāh.
The One without joy or sorrow, Allāh.
The One who rules alone, Allāh.
The One with peace, the qualities of truth and compassion,
You are Allāh.
Allāhu, Allāh, One without anyone else, You are Allāh.
The One who asks about good and evil
on the Day of Questioning, Allāh.
The One who feeds us day and night, Allāh.
The Creator, the Protector, the Nurturer who protects, Allāh.
O most able, great One who resplends everywhere, Allāh.
Allāhu, Allāh, the Treasure without anyone else,
You are Allāh.
Allāhu, Allāh, the Treasure without anyone else,
You are Allāh.


He is the One without food or sleep, Allāh.
He is the One who
cannot be controlled by anything, Allāh.
He is the One who
is eternally omnipresent everywhere, Allāh.

Eternally omnipresent, O God, You alone are Allāh.
Allāhu Allāh, the Treasure without anyone else, Allāh.
Allāhu Allāh, the Treasure without anyone else, Allāh.
The One who helps the helper, Allāh.
The One who is the help which is everywhere, Allāh.
The One who heals all the karma and illnesses, Allāh.
The One who takes to the shore all who are holding on
to the ultimate destination, Allāh.
The One who does not work for wages, Allāh.
The One who serves without selfishness, Allāh.

Who is like Him in this world? Allāh!
Is there a God like Him? Allāh!
Allāhu, Allāh, the Treasure without anyone else,
You are Allāh.
The Treasure without anyone else, You are Allāh.
You are One with Your word, Allāh.
You are the resplendent,
great One in the place of testing, Allāh.
You are the One who bestows grace upon those who
love you, O God, Allāh.
You are the One who gives us food in *ādi* and *anādi*,[1]
and who takes us to the shore, Allāh.
Allāhu, Allāh, the Treasure without anyone else,
You alone are Allāh.

*Al-ḥamdu lillāhi.*
You are yā Rabbal-'ālamīn.

---

1. *ādi* (n.) the primal beginning; *anādi* (n.) the state of darkness before the
beginning

*Qul Huwallāhu Ahad.*
*Allāhus-Samad.*
*Lam yalid:*
*Wa lam yūlad.*
*Wa lam yakul-lahu.*
*Kufuwan ahad.*[2]

Allāhu!

*Al-ḥamdu lillāhi.*
*Rabbil-'ālamīn.*
*Ar-Raḥmānir-Rahīm.*
*Māliki yaumid-dīn.*
*Iyyaka na'budu wa iyyāka nasta'īn.*
*Iḥdinas-sirātal-mustaqīm.*
*Sirātal-ladhīna.*
*An'amta 'alaihim.*
*Ghairil-maghdūbi 'alaihim wa lad-dāllīn.*[3] Āmīn.
Āmīn, āmīn, yā Rabbal-'ālamīn.

Completion in the world of pure souls, *'ālamul-arwāh.*
The One who dwells as the Heart within the heart.
The Light that has settled onto everything, everywhere.
The One who is the Resonance known as illAllāhu,
the Bliss of Grace.
As the Light of the Eye within the eye.

---

2. *Sūratul-Ikhlās,* the Chapter of Purity in the Qur'ān. See Glossary for the translation.
3. *Sūratul-Fātihah,* the opening chapter of the Qur'ān. See Glossary for the translation.

As the Beauty that transcends imagination.
As the Treasure without beginning or end.
You are the eternally Pure One, our yā Rabbal-'ālamīn.

Within the five and the six there is the Golden One,
shining everywhere as the resplendence of Nūr Muhammad,
as the Rahmah that transcends the embryo and the body,
yā Rabbal-'ālamīn who protects and nurtures everywhere.

Allāhu, Allāhu, Allāhu.
The One who is in the world of pure souls and
everywhere, Allāhu.
Understanding as *Qalb* within *qalb*, Allāhu.
The Almighty One who dispels our karma, Allāhu.
The One who is complete as the Heart within the heart,
Allāhu.
The Ruler and Protector of our three worlds, Allāhu.
The One who fills the world of the souls and
everywhere, Allāhu.
The One who gives us the *īmān* which is like nectar and
who fills us with it, Allāhu.

*Āmīn. Āmīn*, yā Rabbal-'ālamīn, Allāhu.
The Absolute Completion who is everywhere,
resonating, shining, explaining, understanding
on the path of the heart, Allāhu.
The One beyond our thoughts, Allāhu.
The One exalted in wisdom, Allāhu.
The One who gives the sounds and
words of *gnānam*, Allāhu.

The Qudrah, the Power, yā Rabbal-ʿālamīn,
He is One, Allāhu.
The Honey intermingled within Love, Allāhu.

The One who lovingly performs prayer and *ibādah*
with good conduct and obedience, Allāhu.
The One who helps His followers, Allāhu.
Tell me, what else can His *ummah,* His followers, speak of
other than Him, Allāhu?
He is the only One filled with peace and
the qualities of truth,
He is the only One who can perform His duty
which is a blessing.
He is the only One who helps in a state of unity.
Is there anyone else in all the worlds like Him?
Is there any God other than Him?

Think of Allāhu.
I am telling you to have certitude and
to do duty in the state of *īmān* in Allāhu,
the God who melts the heart,
the Almighty One who protects us during all our days,
the God who is complete in love.
Pray to Him with *adab,* good conduct,
with the focus and intention of your worship and
*ibādah* directed at Him,
the great Light known as Ādi Param,
the beautiful state that shines in the heart,
the Creator who exists as the Light within the eye.
To all who see Him, He will be
the Resonance within *dīn,* purity.

Say this without saying this in your *qalb*.
It is shining there, explaining in the Nūr.
Look into Him with love and say in your *qalb* that
there is nothing other than Him, the
Almighty One that fills the heart,
God, beloved and exalted.
God, intermingled within *īmān* as
the Word within the word.
Say, illAllāhu.
Search for eternal success.
Focus on the path of bliss.

Always recite that there is nothing other than Him.
Always recite.
There is a sound beyond sound.
His resonance is in that place.
His explanation is in the *qalb*.
He is the Creator beyond the mind.
Recite, recite every day, that there is
no one other than He who is One.
Have certitude and determination of *īmān*.
This will become the good path.

He will protect you day and night.
He will perform the action before we can say the word.
He will dispel all our inherited and
acquired evils and sins.
The God of this completion
will always bring you success.
To have *īmān* with true determined certitude is *dīn*.
To have this with certitude is *dīn*.

Allāhu, Allāhu, Allāhu!
He is One without anyone else, Allāhu.
He is the Eternal, the Eternal, Allāhu.
He is the Loving One, He is Allāhu.
*Āmīn. Āmīn.* Yā Rabbal-'ālamīn.
May it be so. May it be so.
O Creator of All the Universes.

# Alone

*Friday, July 19, 1974*

WE GO ALONE.
No one will go with us.
We have come alone.
I have come alone.
We will go alone.
We live alone.
What should we do?
What should we do?

I think of God every day.
I cry and cry and tears flow from my eyes.
I think of God every day.
I cry and cry and tears flow from my eyes.

We came here alone,
we live here alone,
and in the future we will go alone.
Who will help us?
Who will help us?
Who will come with me to help me?
Who will help us?
Who will come with me?

No one in this birth,
no one in this birth,
since the day I was born,
no one has ever helped me at all.
There has been no help at all.

We will carry out good and evil deeds,
and then on that Day someone
will ask us about them.
No one will take any of
the sins I committed.
No one will support me,
no one will take any of my sins.

Good and evil are
entirely under our control.
What will happen tomorrow and
what I will get
is my responsibility.
No one will help us.
There is no help there.

We are born alone,
we live alone,
and we go alone,
we go alone.

No one will take the burden of our
sins and good deeds.
In this birth,
no one will take

the burden of sin from us.
Not our mother, not our father,
not any of our brothers and sisters
will take it from us.

The burden of what I have done is
carried on my own head.
I have to pick it up and carry it;
there is no one who will take it from me.
Who knows what will happen tomorrow?
Who knows what will happen tomorrow?
Who will help us?
Who will help us?
Has anyone been born who will take our burden?
No one will come forward to do that in this birth.
No one will come forward to do that in this birth.

It is my birth.
The birth I have taken is entirely alone.
Alone in the womb,
alone in the embryo,
born alone,
living alone,
I will go alone.

Will anyone come with me?
Will anyone come with any of us?
Will anyone come with us?
We ourselves have to go there alone.
We have to go alone.

Jean, will anyone come with us?
We are alone in the grave.
We are alone in the grave.
We are alone in the house.
We are alone in the cage of the body.
We are alone in the embryo.
We are alone in the embryo.

We are alone in the cage of the body.
Here in the house we are alone.
We are alone in the grave,
and we have to go,
we have to go there.

There we have no relatives,
no help, no possessions,
no mother, no father, no brothers or sisters —
no one to help us there.
No one will help us, Jean.

We go alone.
We live alone.
We have been born alone.
Our lives here are alone.
What is the benefit in this?
What have we seen in all this?

What belongs to us here?
What ties do we have here?
What attachments do we have here?

There is no help in any of it.
None of it is worth anything.
These attachments are not worth anything.

As soon as the Angel of Death comes,
everyone runs, everyone runs.
No one will ever come with us.
No one will ever come with us.

Even though we cry and cry,
we will have to go.
We will have to take all
the beatings and the blows
we will be given there.
We ourselves will have to
carry the load of
our sins and good deeds.
Each of us, each of us
must carry our own load.

In the end,
we will have to hand over
both the good and the evil
to be weighed;
we will have to hand them over
to be weighed.

We will have to account for
the profit and the loss for
His Questioning, for
the Reckoning.

We will have to
hand in our accounts.
We will have to
hand in our accounts.

After that,
we will have to accept
the punishment for all
our karma, our sins, and our evils.
We will have to accept all
the blows, the kicks, the punches,
the blows, the kicks, the punches,
the cuts and the pummeling.
We will have to accept it all.
We will have to accept it all.

No one will ever listen to this,
no one will even come to give us a little help.
We are the ones who have to suffer.
What can we do?
This is the world.

# Allāh, Allāh,
# There Is No Place You Are Not

*[Faqir's Song]*

*Friday, September 6, 1974, 8:00 A.M.*

You ARE COMPLETE everywhere, Allāh.
You are complete everywhere, Allāh.
You are complete everywhere, Allāh.
You are complete everywhere, Allāh.
There is no place You are not.
There is no place You are not.
There is no One like You.
There is no God like You, Allāh.
There is no One like You.
You are complete everywhere, Allāh.
You are complete everywhere, Allāh.

You are the One who dwells in all lives.
You alone, Allāh.
You are the One who dwells in all lives.
You alone, Allāh.
You are the One who dwells in all lives.
You alone, Allāh.
You alone, Allāh.
You alone, Allāh.
There is no place You are not.
There is no God like You.

There is no place You are not.
There is no God like You.

You are the Light that fills all the universes, Allāh.
You are the Light that fills all the universes, Allāh.
You are the Almighty One without *ādi* and *anādi,* Allāh,
without the beginning and
the darkness before the beginning.
You are the Almighty One without *ādi* and *anādi,* Allāh.
You are the One who dwells everywhere, Allāh.
You are the only One who dwells everywhere, Allāh.
You are the only One who dwells in all lives, Allāh.
You are the only One who dwells in all lives, Allāh.
There is no place You are not.
There is no place You are not.
There is no place You are not.

There is no God like You.
There is no God like You, Allāh, Allāh.
You are the One most exalted in love, Allāh.
You are the One most exalted in love, Allāh.
You are the only One who regards everyone
with equality, Allāh.
You are the only One who regards everyone
with equality, Allāh.
You are the Protector and Nourisher of all lives, Allāh.
You are the Protector and Nourisher of all lives, Allāh.

You alone are Allāh.
You alone are Allāh.

You alone are Allāh.
You shine and completely fill everything.
You shine and completely fill everything.
You are God, Allāh.
Allāh, Allāh.
Everything is Allāh, Allāh.
You are the One who dwells in all lives, Allāh, Allāhu.
There is no place You are not.

There is no God like You.
There is no God like You.
You are the One intermingled
in our food and our nourishment.
You are the One sealed
in our lives and our bodies.
You are the One who shines forth
from love and from wisdom.
You are the Almighty One who rules all the worlds.
You are the Almighty One who rules all the worlds.
You are the Almighty One who rules all the worlds.

Allāh.
You alone are Allāh.
You alone are Allāh.
Allāh, Allāh.
You are the Omnipresence in all lives, Allāh.
You are the Omnipresence in all lives, Allāh.
There is no place You are not, Allāh.
There is no place You are not, Allāh.
There is no One, no God like You, Allāh.

You are the only One without beginning or end, Allāh.
You are the only One without beginning or end, Allāh.
You are the One who treats everyone with equality, Allāh.
You are the One who treats everyone with equality, Allāh.
You are the One who destroys our sins, Allāh.
You are the One who destroys our sins, Allāh.
You are the One who protects and watches over us.
You are Allāh.
You are the One who protects and watches over us.
You are Allāh.

You are the jeweled Light within the eye
that watches everything, Allāh.
You are the jeweled Light within the eye
that watches everything, Allāh.
You are the Almighty, Compassionate Protector, Allāh.
You are the Almighty, Compassionate Protector, Allāh.
You are the Almighty Protector, Allāh.
Allāh, Allāh.
There is no God like You, Allāh.
You are the Omnipresence in all lives, Allāh.
You are the Omnipresence in all lives, Allāh.

You are the only One, the Omnipresence that
shines everywhere.
Allāh.
You are the only One, the Omnipresence that
shines everywhere.
Allāh.
There is no One who helps like You, Allāh.

There is no place You are not, Allāh.
There is no place You are not, Allāh.
There is no God like You, Allāh.
There is no God like You.
There is no one like You in the world or anywhere, Allāh.
Allāh, Allāh.

You are the only Omnipresence in all lives, Allāh.
There is no place You are not, Allāh.
There is no place You are not, Allāh.
There is no other God like You, Allāh.
You are the Almighty One, Allāh.
You are God who does what is fair and just, Allāh.
You are the One who does what is fair and just, Allāh.
You are the eternal Ruler, Allāh.
You are the eternal Ruler, Allāh.
Allāh, Allāh.
You are the only One who is the Omnipresence in
all lives, Allāh.
There is no place You are not, Allāh.
There is no place You are not, Allāh.
There is no God like You, Allāh.
There is no God like You, Allāh.

You are the only One who dwells within me, Allāh.
You are the only One who dwells within my body, Allāh.
You are the One who gives explanations
as the Life within my life, Allāh.
You are the One who gives explanations
as the Life within my life, Allāh.

On the open path, You are the One who shows the
complete path, Allāh.
On the open path, You are the One who shows the
complete path, Allāh.
You are the One who eternally exists, Allāh.
You are the One who does not deviate from truth and
who rules alone, Allāh.
Allāh, Allāh, Allāh, Allāh.
You are the only One who is the Omnipresence in all lives.
You are the only One who is the Omnipresence in all lives.
There is no place You are not, Allāh.
There is no place You are not, Allāh.
There is no God like You, Allāh.
There is no God like You, Allāh.

You are the Almighty One
who melts the heart, Allāh.
You are the Almighty One who melts
the mind within our hearts.
You are the One who shows us how to dispel the
tricks of the mind, Allāh.
You are the One who shows us how to dispel the
tricks of the mind, the Clear One, Allāh.
Allāh, Allāh, Allāh, Allāh.
Allāh, Allāh.

You are the Omnipresence in all lives,
the only One, Allāh.
You are the One beyond
race, religions, and separations, Allāh.

You are the One beyond
race, religions, and separations, Almighty Allāh.
You are the great Ruler, the Master of Divine Wisdom,
the Almighty Allāh.
You are the great Ruler, the Master of Divine Wisdom,
the Almighty Allāh.
You dwell within us as the One within the One, Allāh.
You are the One intermingled in all lives, Allāh.
You are the One intermingled in all lives, Allāh.
Allāh, Allāh.

You are the only One who is the Omnipresence in
all lives, Allāh.
There is no place You are not, Allāh.
There is no place You are not, Allāh.
There is no God like You.
You are the Almighty One, Allāh.
There is no God like You.
You are the Almighty One, You are Allāh.

You are the Resplendence
without name or country, Allāh.
You are the Resplendence
without name or country, Allāh.
You have no parents, no relatives, no birth, no birth.
You are the Resplendence, Allāh.
You are the One who dwells within the truth as
a Resplendence,
the only One, Allāh.

You are the One who dwells within the truth as
a Resonance, the only One, Allāh.
Allāh, Allāh, Allāh, Allāh.
Allāh, Allāh.

You are the Omnipresence in all lives,
the only One, Allāh.
You are the Omnipresence in all lives,
the only One, Allāh.
There is no place You are not, Allāh.
There is no place You are not, Allāh.
There is no God like You anywhere in the world,
Almighty One, Allāh.

You are the endless resplendent Light without
name or birth, Allāh.
You are the endless, resplendent Light without
name or birth, Allāh.
You are the One without the madness that
arises from the bile, Allāh.
You are the One who is filled with the resonance of
absolute Truth,
You alone are Allāh.
You are the One who is filled with the resonance of
absolute Truth,
You alone are Allāh.
Allāh, Allāh, Allāh, Allāh.

You are the Omnipresence in all lives.
You alone are Allāh.
You are the Omnipresence in all lives.
You alone are Allāh.
There is no place You are not, Allāh.
There is no place You are not.

Almighty One, Allāh.
There is no God like You in the world, Allāh.
There is no other God like You in the world, Allāh.
You are the resplendent Light
without birth or destruction.
You are the Truth of the Resplendent Grace
that knows and understands
what lies within, Allāh.

You are the sound and the resonance in the heart,
the Resonant One, the only One, Allāh.
Your form is that of peaceful truth,
patience, tolerance, and tranquility.
You exist as the Atom within the atom.
You resonate as Wisdom within wisdom.
You transcend *ādi* and *anādi*.

You are the most wondrous thing, Allāh.
You are the One who resplends with
indivisible and absolute completion.
You are the state of bliss, Allāh,
the state of bliss, Allāh.

You are our state of bliss, Allāh.
Allāh.
You are the state of bliss, Allāh.
Allāh, Allāh, Allāh, Allāh.
You are the Omnipresence in all lives, Allāh.
There is no place You are not, Allāh.
There is no God like You, Allāh.

No name, no birth, no end, no destruction,
no beginning, no end,
no earth, no sky, nothing hidden,
no water, no fire, no air, no water,
nothing to stand upon,
no destruction, no end.
You are the One beyond the beginning and the end.
You are the indivisible and absolute
Treasure of Completion,
Allāh, Allāh.

You are the Treasure that gives without diminishing,
no matter how much we take and take from it, Allāh.
You are the form that gives and gives without diminishing
to all lives inside the heart.
Indivisible and absolute Completion, Allāh.
For this world and the next,
You are the Completion of the Heart
that gives and gives without diminishing.

You are the eternal Treasure, Allāh.
You are the Resonance of truth,
existing alone,
the One who rules alone,
the peaceful Quality of Truth that contains nothing else.
As the Word with the word,
as the Grace with the grace,
You are the One who explains as the Resonance.
You are the One who explains as the Resonance.

Light of Divine Wisdom, Allāh.
Light of Divine Wisdom, Allāh.
Allāh, Allāh.
You are the only One who is the Omnipresence in
all lives, Allāh.
There is no place You are not, Allāh.
There is no place You are not, Allāh.
There is no God like You,
Almighty One, Allāh.
There is no other God like You,
Almighty One, Allāh.

You are the Treasure that transcends religions and
scriptures, Allāh.
You are the Treasure that transcends religions and
scriptures, Allāh.
You are the Power beyond race,
religion, and separation.
Almighty One, Allāh.

The Atom within the atom,
the Life within life,
the Heart within the heart.

You dwell openly inside,
teaching grace,
the clear Treasure within wisdom, Allāh.
O God, indivisible and absolute Completion,
You dwell intermingled with love.

You are the wonder,
the wonder, Allāh,
the wonder, Allāh.
You dwell inside the lives of all the atoms, Allāh.
You dwell inside the lives of all the atoms, Allāh.
There is no place You are not, Allāh.
There is no place You are not, Allāh.
There is no other God like You.

Almighty One, Allāh.
There is no other God like You,
Almighty One, Allāh.

# Easy to Talk About

EVERYONE CAN SAY THINGS in the world,
so many things.
Everyone can say things.
But the mouth has no fidelity.
The eyes have no screen.
The nose has no veil.
The ears have no forbearance.
The legs have no control.
The hands have no restraint.
The mind has no reverence.

Everyone can say things in the world,
so many things.
The ears have no filter.
The eyes have no screen.
The nose has no veil.
The tongue has no control.
The hands have no restraint.
The feet have no stability.
The *qalb*, the heart, has no submission.
The heart has no submission.

The state of the mind
has no place in which to stand,
no place in which to be.

Everyone can say things in the world,
so many things.
So what is wrong with that?
What is wrong with that?
It is that it is difficult and rare to act
according to the way you speak.
It is difficult and rare.
In his life, a man can say anything,
absolutely anything.

He can also act in many ways
during the days of his life.
He can hit.
He can give or he can take with his hands.
He can criticize and he can curse, or
he can trust and speak with love and
comfort others with his tongue.
His nose—he can act without awareness
of what is
good and what is bad.
He can speak ignorantly with his mouth.

His eyes can look at glitters and maya
without differentiating
between the truth and falsehood in them.
He can listen to everything he hears with his ears.

He can enjoy it all.
He can embrace it all.
He can listen to and experience all the happiness
and sadness that come to him.

He can say anything.
He can know anything.
He can look at anything.
He can smell anything.
He can give anything.
He can walk anywhere.
He can do anything.
But to know the good and the evil,
to understand it with *pahut arivu,*
with divine analytic wisdom,
to differentiate between truth and falsehood,
to walk on the path of truth —
that is difficult and rare.
That is difficult and rare, difficult and rare.

He can become a swami.
He can act like a mendicant.
He can wander about like a yogi.
He can wear a dot of red ochre on his forehead.
He can carry a brass kettle.
He can grow a beard.
He can twirl his mustache.
He can grow the hair on his head.
He can grow a bushel of hair in his armpits.
He can grow hair everywhere.

But if he does not understand the meaning
of having a pure heart,
if he keeps one thing in his heart,
another thing in his mouth,
another thing in his demeanor,
another thing in his actions—
he can do this.
He can do anything he wants.
But to know that one truth, to be clear,
and to act accordingly is difficult and rare,
it is difficult and rare.

He can wear a dot of red ochre on his forehead.
He can carry a brass kettle.
He can twirl his mustache.
He can grow his beard.
He can obtain titles.
He can obtain honors and degrees.
He can wear emblems of piety.
He can walk about in robes.
He can act with lust, hatred, miserliness,
greed, fanaticism, and envy.
He can nurture all the six evils.
He can nurture arrogance, karma, and maya.
He can indulge in intoxicants, lust, theft,
murder, and falsehood.
He can look at the fourteen worlds of maya
and keep them all in his heart.
He can hide them all there.
He can live like a tiger in a sheepskin.

He can walk about and
the world will never know.
He can do anything he wants.
But to understand that
there is one God who does exist,
to know that truth and
to understand its inner meaning
is difficult and rare, difficult and rare,
difficult and rare.

He can wear a dot of red ochre,
he can wear signs of piety,
and display all of the attendant qualities,
but to have God's Qualities,
to know how to open your heart,
to have modesty, reserve, respect for others, and
fear of wrongdoing
is difficult and rare.
It is difficult and rare, it is difficult and rare.

To think countless thoughts and
to keep them hidden inside,
to fill your heart with the form of darkness,
to fill your heart with desire and
thoughts of your wife, children, and possessions,
to keep them in a net of ignorance
in your heart—
you can do that.
You can wear signs of piety on the outside.
You can act as if others see only that.

You can obtain
all the titles, honors, and degrees,
you can act without knowing the difference between
sin and virtue.
This is the state of man.
It is easy to say what he says.
But to act accordingly is difficult and rare.
It is easy to say things.
But to act accordingly is difficult and rare,
difficult and rare.

God who is One does exist.
His state and His qualities do exist.
He rules in a state of love.
He loves other lives as His own life.
He trusts other lives.
He protects others as He protects Himself.
He does duty without talking about it.
He gives grace without the need
for friendships or relationships.
He acts with the Three Thousand Qualities of Grace.
He rules as a Power without selfishness.
He protects all lives:
earth lives, fire lives, water lives, air lives,
the lives in the ether,
and the light lives.
He protects and feeds the six kinds of lives with love.
Ādi, the great Light, that is His state.

To know this and to act accordingly is
difficult and rare.
It is easy to speak of it, but to know it and
to act accordingly is difficult and rare.
To know this and to act accordingly is
difficult and rare.
To wear dots of red ochre,
to grow your beard and mustache is very easy.
It is easy to become a swami.
But to have the qualities of peace and truth, and
to act with God's actions is difficult and rare,
difficult and rare, difficult and rare.

To nurture religion, to spread religion is easy;
to beg in many ways,
to point out signs of piety,
to obtain titles, honors, and degrees,
to join with the three pieces of excrement that are
arrogance, karma, and maya is easy.
To gather the six evils and the three qualities
that came before —
three times two are the forces
that come to rule you,
along with the five who are
the enemies of the heart —
to keep those in your heart,
saying, "You are different from me.
I am different from you,"
to have the separations of race and religion,

to keep the qualities of God's Power
in ignorance,
to make your heart dark,
to turn every place where God could be into the
darkness of ignorance,
to turn the whole body—nerves, skin, flesh,
bones, and blood—
into darkness,
to focus on titles and honors,
to become entangled in the evils of karma,
to look for a way—this is what man does.

It is easy to say things.
But to act accordingly,
to know and understand the truth and to act
accordingly is difficult and rare,
it is difficult and rare.

To act according to the fashion of the times,
he changes his form in many ways.
He forgets the destiny that God has given him
and searches for karma.
To follow his relatives, his friends, and
his blood ties,
to act according to what they tell him to do,
to be a swami with a red dot,
to gain titles, honors, praise, and positions,
this is what man will do.

O man, know this state.
All of his thoughts will take form
in the darkness of ignorance.
He will triumph in hell.
He will nurture the separations of religion.
He will have many differences.
He will appear to be a man,
but his qualities will be like those of an animal,
and he will walk in the darkness of maya.

What he says is easy for him to say.
It is easy to speak with the mouth.
But to understand the truth and act accordingly is
difficult and rare, difficult and rare,
difficult and rare.

# The Way to the Kingdom

*Monday, January 27, 1975, 9:00 A.M.*

*[Bawa Muhaiyaddeen☺ told us to play this song over and over again.]*

IN THE PRESENCE OF HE who is One,
why would we be afraid in the world?
In the presence of He who is One,
why would we be afraid?
In the presence of He who is One,
why would we be afraid?
Why would we be afraid?

In the presence of
the eternal Treasure, the outspread grace,
the eternal Treasure, the outspread grace,
the undiminishing wealth,
why would we be afraid?
Why would we be afraid?

If we believe, then His grace will belong to us.
If we believe, then His grace will belong to us.
If we focus on it, the goodness will be ours.
If we focus on it, the goodness will be ours.
O loving ones, O trusting ones,

O loving ones, O trusting ones,
if we embrace Him in a state of love,
what will we lack?

Even though the times are changing,
our Creator who is One will never change.
If all of us become one in the truth,
and if we embrace Him,
what will we lack?

O humankind, join together as one,
search for the grace of God.
O humankind, come here,
join together as one, and
merge with the One.
That is the state,
that is what will bring the undiminishing wealth,
that is what exists within love and trust.
It is God who brings the grace.

Focus on Him.
Search for Him.
Join with Him, and
sing to Him in a state of love.

O loving ones,
you who have been born with me!
Because you are the children of one Mother,
pay constant obeisance to
the Eternal and the Absolute,

the Almighty One,
with the qualities of the plenitude,
without missing a moment in time,
without forgetting for a moment in time.

He is Ādi.
He is the great Light,
He is the great King of Justice who rules in the heart.
To those who are good and to everyone,
He is the One who gives love and unfailing justice.
Think of Him and melt,
search for Him in your *qalb,* your heart.
Search within the truth for the love of He who is One.
If your heart opens,
and if that becomes complete within you,
you will obtain the grace of God.

The state of separation is the path of doubt.
The state of separation is the path of doubt.
You must cut this completely out of your minds.
You must bow in truth to He who is One
and think of the One who rules inside and outside.

Search for Him.
All of you, join together and
sing with the King who rules the three worlds.
He is the Almighty One.
He is the One who exists forever.
In your life and in your body,
He is the loving One.

He is the One who will always help us.
He is the loving One in both worlds.
He is the One who bestows the grace,
the One who provides the nectar.
That Compassion is God.
He is the God who protects us,
our beloved God,
the God who rules us.

That Treasure is the Treasure that will exist forever.
That Treasure is what rules us and
bestows the grace.
That Treasure is intermingled with wisdom.
He is the God who lives forever.
If we search for Him in our hearts,
what will we ever lack?

Jeweled lights of my eyes,
my lights of grace,
O true ones who have been born with me,
all of you, join together as one,
call out to God,
say the name of God,
open your hearts,
direct all your love and affection towards Him and sing.

You must always live as the loving ones.
You must always focus on His state of grace.
You have to live in the truth
and walk in the world,

accepting only His help.
Your lives must be lived in the state of justice;
your lives must be lived in the state of justice;
you must live in this way always.

There is no wonder in our existence other than God,
the great and glorious One.
We have been born in order to know that.
We have come here in order to live within Ādi,
the great One.
We have come here in order to eat His food, always.

In order to realize this state,
you have to open your heart
and stand within it.
All lives must become one and live together there.

Other lives must be like your life.
You have to realize this in a state of equality.
The hunger of others must be like your own hunger.
The hunger of others must be like your own hunger.
You have to be clear about this and know this
in your feeling and in your awareness,
and you have to act accordingly.
The sadness of others must be your own sadness.
You have to realize this and
act according to the divine words of your Father.

We must live as one in this exquisite state,
imbibing the nectar of His grace,

with certainty, with absolute conviction,
you and I
becoming one life,
dwelling intermingled in love,
establishing ourselves in the state of grace,
dwelling clearly in wisdom,
living in love as one form.

In this eternal life,
if we never deviate from absolute truth,
what more would we ever need?
What would ever make us sad?
What poverty or difficulty would we ever experience?

Justice and fairness must become the
actions in our lives.
We think our belongings and our relatives belong to us,
but it is only ignorance, and we have to destroy it.
We have to gather all lives into our love,
and know that we are all one blood,
one blood, one attachment,
one mother, one father.

Ādi is the great Light:
it is the state of grace in which God resplends.
With trust and with love,
with faith, certitude, and determination,
we have to place this state
into our wisdom,
into feeling, awareness, intellect, and

our sense of judgment;
we have to know this with wondrous wisdom.

With compassion, we have to distinguish and look at,
we have to distinguish and look at
the happiness and sadness of all lives.
If we distinguish between good and evil,
knowing the difference,
realizing it, and acting accordingly,
our Father who is God
will be in front of us and behind us.

In truth, He is inside and outside.
He rules as One, and He knows.
If we know Him as justice,
eternal life will be ours:
it is certain that we will be able to reach
the grace of the Unique One.

Jeweled lights of my eyes,
all who have been born with me,
creations of God,
our God is the most dear One,
the One who belongs to us,
our Rabbil-'ālamīn,
Lord of the universes,
the One who exists eternally as Truth.
He is the One alone who
bestows assistance from within all lives.

He is the One who bestows the grace as compassion.
He is the Protector beyond the imagination of the mind.
He is God, the Eternal.
If you think of Him in your heart with determination
and bow down before Him,
the entire world will become good.
There is no poverty in His kingdom.

Jeweled lights of my eyes,
you who have been born with me
in the creation of my Creator,
dear ones,
as your birthright,
your qualities must exist
within the qualities of God.
O my dearest creations in this birth,
you must remain within His qualities;
they are your birthright.

If you are glorious in compassion,
think of your Father,
and live your lives with integrity,
what sorrow will there be for you?
You can reach the grace of the One who is alone.

This is what my dear Father has said so exquisitely;
this is what my dear Father has said so exquisitely,
and this birthright must never change.
We must think of the meaning
of the words of God, the Creator,
and act accordingly.

If we act quickly,
our words and our actions in the same state,
what more will we ever need?

If we are the action within the action,
our lives will be intermingled with His grace.
If our qualities settle into His qualities, and
if we dwell in His compassion,
what sadness will we ever have?

If you act with
the compassion, the love, and the justice
of our Father, the Creator, with
the integrity, the patience, the tranquility,
the peace, and the justice of absolute truth—
if you do this as your birthright,
what sadness will you ever have in this world?

O my dearest children,
my very own,
jeweled lights of my eyes,
creations dwelling in my heart,
lives intermingled with all lives,
my creations intermingled with the truth,
you must live as the trusted ones.

You must obtain the help of He who is One.
You must think of this,
know this deeply and thoroughly,
and act accordingly.

O my eyes,
O my gems,
O my creations of compassion and love,
there is one God who is yours by birthright.
He protects you inside and outside.
He is the One who is exquisite,
compassionate, and patient.
He is the primal Father,
the One to whom you must pray.

If you leave all racial and religious prejudice behind,
if you leave all racial and religious prejudice behind,
He will bestow the power of His compassion upon you.
God who is your birthright
is the Almighty One who belongs equally to everyone,
the One who dwells in and owns the abode of the soul.

He is the One who rules justly.
He is the One who is always fair.
He is the One alone who never deviates from truth.
He is the One who has the peaceful qualities of truth.

As your birthright,
it is through compassion and with trust
that you must pray,
that you must obtain the grace of the trusted One.

Come, come, creations,
come join together, join together,

come here to
search, search for what is good
on the good path!
Focus, focus on His qualities in your life!

You must constantly and eternally pray to
the patient One who rules with compassion,
to the One who knows the heart with justice.
It is a certainty in your life
that you must act
with the qualities of
He who is One.
Your words and your actions have to be in the same state.
You have to do this ceaselessly.
Then the grace of God who lives as love
will become the wealth of your compassion.

It is this state that you must realize,
it is in this state that you must act,
jeweled lights of my eyes
creations in my heart,
jeweled lights who are my birthright.

You must dispel the rationalization for all separation.
You must reach the path on which there is no rebirth.
You must act in the life that is your birthright.
You must live by never seeking any help other than His.
If you do this,
what sadness can ever come to you in the world?

The duties of the justice of the King and
the patience of God's justice
are part of the birthright of the family of humankind.
This is the sovereign state of the blessing of
the One alone:
the state of peace, the qualities of truth,
the state of patience.

If you are clear about them [the qualities] with wisdom,
if you act accordingly,
if you bow down before God
and no one else,
the life that is our birthright will be exalted,
and truly,
His compassion, His blessing, and His grace will
be complete.

Come, look at this.
Come, realize this, and search for the grace.
Look at it in this world and in the next realm.
Make this world into God's world.

Put your own heart out,
bring God inside and make Him your own.
Make His qualities and actions your life.
Make the Guru and the Grace complete there.
Then live without happiness or sadness;
that will make your life complete.

O my beloved, O my state,
jeweled lights of my eyes,

creations filled with grace and born with me,
if you truly realize this state,
what sadness will you have in this world?
Where you live will be the kingdom of God.
The knowledge of this *is* the kingdom of God.

If you understand,
you can push aside the kingdom of hell,
saying, "Leave me!"
You can find the kingdom of your birthright within
the truth.
If you realize this and act accordingly,
it will be God's kingdom.
If you live in God's kingdom,
what sadness is there in the world of God?
If the truth fills you,
what worldly illusion,
poverty, or illness will there be?

Realize this state, my child.
Have love for all lives, my child.
Love the lives of others as your own life.
To do this and live in the world,
is a life of grace.
The life of grace is the life of a human being.
His actions will be the birthright of the good life.
The qualities and what is in the heart are one life,
the exalted good life of the grace of Khudā, God.

Realize this, my children,
be unwavering in this world and in the next realm.

Do not be afraid of poverty and illness.
Take refuge in God's love every day of your life.
If you regard this as your plenitude,
if you stay there in that truth,
what sadness can you have?
*Āmīn. Āmīn.*
May it be so. May it be so.

# When We Sing About God

*Monday, June 30, 1975, 12:55 P.M.*

HERE, IN THIS PLACE, we should sing only songs about God—
say it without saying it, sing without singing it, and speak
without speaking. Aye? *Enna?*[1] That is how it should be done.

> We must sing meltingly
> without allowing the mind to melt.
> We must sing meltingly
> without allowing the mind to melt,
> and place God who is the Bliss of Grace
> into love within love.
> This must be our intention.
>
> Place God who is the Bliss of Grace
> into love within love.
> This must be the intention in our hearts.
> You and I must sing in unison of
> the Treasure that is complete.
> You and I must sing in unison of
> the Treasure that is complete.
> Without the sixty-four arts,

---

1. *enna* (interjection) [Lit. what] Don't you agree?

the compassionate art of the Creator
must come and flow from us.
We must connect with the compassionate loving art
of the Creator and then sing.

This song must melt the hearts of all lives.
This song must melt the hearts of all lives.
The Grace of God must come into and
flow from those hearts.
The Grace of God must come into and
flow from those hearts.
The state of love must overflow there.
The state of love must overflow there.
The love of our original Father,
the love of our original Father must intermingle there.
It must intermingle there.

The Light of wisdom must come,
and it must shine there.
The Light of wisdom must come,
and it must shine there.
We who are the loving ones,
we who are the loving ones
must become one body
and intermingle
as life within life,
as life within life,
as One within One,
as God within God.
We must intermingle as God within God.

We must sing
in the state of compassionate love,
the state of compassionate love.
We must sing so that the maya of the world
does not intermingle with us.
We must sing in a way so that the maya of the world
does not intermingle with us.
The Grace must flow and dispel the darkness,
so the mind and desire that want to swallow us
are chased away.

We must sing, we must sing
so the mind is driven away,
so the Angel of Death flies away,
so the Angel of Death flies away and we escape,
so the Grace of God resonates,
so the Grace of God resonates,
the heart shines with Light, and
His Grace explains.
Desire for earth, desire for woman,
desire for gold must flee.
Desire for earth, desire for woman,
desire for gold must flee.

The ultimate treasure that is the Grace of God,
the Nūr, the Light, must melt, flow,
give the explanation, resonate, shine,
be taken in, and understood.
It is the Grace of God that must sing there.
Our heart must be Him.

The "I" and the "you" must disappear.
The "I" and the "you" must disappear.
The divine Grace of God must come to sing.
It must come to sing.
This must be understood in all lives.

Sing, sing with the Grace that
must pierce and enter their hearts.
Their hearts must melt and dissolve
and look for He who is One.
The state of love must descend, and
Grace must flow in a state of bliss
as the song of the bliss of Grace.
That is the song.
That is the search for God.
That is the unity of a heavenly life within us.
That is an exalted song.
That is an exalted song.

The intention that dispels the darkness,
the unity that intermingles and dwells with God,
this is how we must sing.
The state of shining Light,
the state of shining Light
will fill the heart, the body, and everything.
We must become Him.

The state of love is the song of bliss.
That is the unity that comes from His grace.
That is the resonant intention that opens the heart.

That is a complete song.
That is what must come to our hearts.
This is what we must understand and sing.
This is what we must sing.
*Āmīn.*
May it be so.

# Why Was I Born in This World?

*Thursday, October 30, 1975, 12:25 P.M.*

WHY WAS I BORN in this world,
in this world, in this world?
Why was I born in this world, in this world?
Why was I born in this world, in this world?
I have no place to stay.
I have no bed in which to sleep.
I have no plate from which to eat.
There is no place for me to sleep, to sit, or to rest.
There is no place for me to sleep, to sit, or to rest.

Why was I born on this earth?
Why was I born on this earth?
O God, why did You create me in this world?
O God, why did You create me?
Why did You create me in this world?

Wherever I look there are wonders.
There are many people who rule this world.
The gaze of their eyes, their goals,
their thoughts, their intentions,
their minds, their qualities, and
their speeches are killing people.

They are tormenting love.
They are making grace run away.
They are driving God away and banishing Him.
They are driving God away and banishing Him.
They are praising ignorance.
They are loving the darkness.
They are doing many, many things like this.

They are dancing.
In the world they are singing "I."
They are playing "mine."
They are reciting, "Everything is in my hands."
They are pointing out the differences between
the "you" and the "I."
They are playing without the wisdom of *gnānam,*
the wisdom of the Divine.

They are singing, they are dancing.
They are singing, they are dancing.
They are playing games with many evils.
They are beating those who think of You.
They are driving away those who know the truth.
They are banishing those who have wisdom.
Blissfully, they search for food for their stomachs.

O God, O Ruler of Grace, the One who is
Incomparable Love,
You are the One who is undiminishing wealth,
undiminishing wealth,
love and compassion,
the One who has these things in completion,

who watches with love,
who protects those who love,
the One who lives in the blissful *qalb*,
in the innermost heart.
O my Creator, my God,
why did You create Your slaves in this world,
on this earth?

O God, in this world You are a compassionate Father,
the One who can destroy all our karma.
O God, O our Father,
the Father who bestows grace,
Father, Beloved One, Most Merciful One,
why did You create me in this world?
Why did You create me in this world?

The more I see, the more frightened I am.
My heart is afraid and trembling.
My heart is dissolving.
My whole body aches.
The light in my eyes is blocked.
The hearing in my ears is listening to this.
All of my faculties are trembling and breaking apart.
Trembling, my senses, my faculties are breaking.
My heart is trembling.
My *qalb* is fading away.
My *qalb* is fading away.
The flower of my heart is fading and falling.
O God, O my Father, why did You create Your slaves
in this world?
Why did You create them in this world?

O You who are our Father!
You must come at this time to
protect the hearts of the poor ones and
grant them Your grace,
protect them and give them that grace.
O Father, O God, jeweled Light of my eyes.
O Father, O God, jeweled Light of my eyes.
The end of the world is approaching.
Here karma, arrogance, impatience, jealousy, treachery,
the "I" and the "you," and their arrogance are
wasting our time.

Without clarity, they are attempting to live like that;
they are attempting to rule the world.
They are attempting to rule this world.
They are attempting to fly into space.
They have studied
how to break apart the sun, the moon, and the stars,
how to break apart the sun, the moon, and the stars.
They have studied
how to break apart the sun, the moon, and the stars.

They took the atom, and with it, they tried to destroy You.
They have forgotten Your grace.
They have lost Your love.
They are attempting to create and destroy
the fetus and the body.
O my God, O my Father,
why did You create me in this world?

You must come to protect Your slaves.
Your compassion is needed here.
You must live in our hearts, our *qalbs,* and
    grant us Your grace.
Your love must come down to us.
You must remove the dangers of the world,
    the accidents, the harmful and evil actions.
O my Father, You must come to us.
You must dwell in our hearts and grant us grace.
Because of all these evils that could come,
You must give us the medicine that can cut them off.
You must give it to us as our birthright.
O my Father, please!

Why did You create us in this world?
Why did You create us in this world?
Why did You create us in this world?
The times have changed.
Man's wisdom has changed.
He has filled himself with darkness
    that covers the *qalb* in his heart.
He has given up his wisdom.
He has filled himself with the state of ignorance.
He has kept arrogant and illusory thoughts in his heart.
He has planted the crops of destruction.
He has planted the crops of destruction.

As a result of this, he has completely dispelled the
    aspects of grace and love.
He has forgotten the truth.

He is imagining the world to be permanent.
He is killing all living beings.
He has driven away Your compassion and Your love.
This state has taken form,
becoming the plants of the world,
becoming the seeds,
becoming darkness.
They [the seeds of darkness] are everywhere like atoms;
they will become fire.
They will become fire, and afterwards destruction.
This is what is occurring now.

O my Father, You must come to us.
You must protect and grant Your grace to
Your slaves, Your slaves.
You must grant Your grace from within our *qalbs*.
O my Creator, O Great One, O my Father,
You must come to us.

Man has flown with these five:
filling himself with earth, fire, water, air, and ether;
he has made a form out of those five.
This man has attempted to rule the three worlds,
the *awwal*, the *dunyā*, and the *ākhirah*.
This man has attempted to rule these three worlds.
He has forgotten You, lost the truth,
driven away compassion,
hidden the deed to the birthright that
comes from his Creator.

He has filled himself with the darkness of satan,
and taken up a life of illusion.
He has made his mind into an animal.
He has blocked his eyesight and his thoughts;
he has blocked his eyesight and his thoughts
with intoxicants.
He has buried himself in darkness.
He has forgotten the state in which he once existed.
Without understanding birth and death,
he is attempting to rule this world.

O my Father, You must come to us.
You must dwell in our hearts and grant us Your grace.
You must protect Your slaves.
O my real Treasure, You are my Father.
You are the God who is Love,
the One who exists eternally as Grace,
the One who knows the completion of the heart,
the One who omnipresently and eternally protects us.

O Primal Father, You must come to us.
You must end the suffering of Your slaves.
You must come to us.
You must come here to us.
You must give us wisdom that is complete.
You must give us the eyes and the Light to see You.
You must grant them to us.
You must grant them to us.

We need the ears to hear Your words,
the nose to smell Your fragrance;
we need Your fragrance,
the good fragrance of love and grace.
So that we may see You and speak to You,
we need the tongue of *imān,* absolute faith.
We need the tongue that knows
the good taste, Your taste.
We need that taste,
the tongue that can sing to You and praise You,
the fragrance that melts into everything
in all the universes,
melting our *qalbs,* melting our minds,
melting all our thoughts,
existing without action
in a state of eternal bliss with You.
We need the completed resplendent heart
in the three worlds.

O my Father,
if we do not get these things,
if You will not give us these things,
why did You create us?
Why did You create us in this earth-world?
Why did You create us in this earth-world?
O God, O my Father!

There is no place for us here.
There is no bed in which to sleep.
There is no land on which to walk.

There is no place in which to dwell.
There is no form, no place, no vision
for a human being here,
O my Creator, except for You.

Your place is our rightful place.
Your kingdom is our birthright.
Your state is permanent.
You are our words and breath.
Your heart is the heart that is the place
for those who live believing in this.

In this world, those who live like that have
no place, no place, no place!
Why did You create us without a place?
Why did You create us in this world
without a place, O my God?

O my Father, You have to give us a place.
O my Father, You have to give us a place in Your heart.
You must grant us the sweetness of Your heart,
the food of Your heart, the fruit of Your heart,
the love of Your heart, the compassion of Your heart,
the justice of Your heart, the truth of Your heart,
the Light of Your heart, the compassion of Your heart,
the duty of Your heart, the gaze of Your heart,
the sound of Your heart, the fragrance of Your heart,
the speech of Your heart, the body of Your heart,
the rules of Your heart, Your decision, and Your kingdom.
O Merciful One! Come to us, grant us Your grace.
You must come to grant us Your grace.

We are living with this hope.
Where is there a place for Your slave in this world?
Where is the place?
Where is the house?
Where is the jungle?
Where is the food?
Here, what is here for him?
What is here for him, where is his place?
There is no place for him here.
Where can he sit? Where can he sit?
Why did You create us in this world?

O my Father,
You are the One who resonates as Allāhu.
Your grace resplends everywhere.
Your work is to make darkness run away,
to make darkness run away,
so that Your Light resplends everywhere,
so that it resonates in all lives.

Food and water, creation and protection
are Your responsibility.
To create and to protect is Your responsibility.
O Most Able One, if You were not going to protect us,
O Most Able One, if You were not going to protect us,
why did You create us in this earth-world?
Why did You create us in this earth-world?

The earth will be destroyed by the fire.
Many things will be destroyed by the air.
Water will cause the hills to become valleys.
Because of the darkness, the rain,
the *nafs,* the desires, the arrogance, the atoms,
the fire, the air, the water, the earth, and the colors,
You have been forgotten.

Because of that arrogance, we stand in peril now,
the state of destruction and the end are here —
destroyed by fire,
crushed and beaten by air,
water rising up from earthquakes, and
finally, finally the world will be destroyed
by the atoms, by the atoms.
The day of destruction and the end
are drawing closer, closer, closer.
Destruction and the end are occurring now, now.

At this time, You must protect us.
You must protect Your servants,
Your slaves, Your children,
those who live in Your land,
those whose hearts are budding and blossoming.
You must protect the children.

O Compassionate Father, You must come to us!
O Compassionate Father, You must come to us!
You must understand the reason and give us Your grace.

You must give us the grace.
O my Father, You must come to us.
At this moment, at this time, this minute,
You must protect us and give us Your grace.
O my Father, jeweled Light of my eye,
You must come to us.

If we look in this direction, there are horrors.
If we look in that direction, there is the destruction.
Wherever we look, Your name is not mentioned.
Wherever we look, there is no love for You.
Wherever we look, there is no one who praises You
or speaks about You.
Even the word "God" is gone.
"His grace" is not present in the world anymore.
Your word, Your name, and Your praise are gone.
In this *dunyā,* this world, they say with arrogance,
"There is no God. I am God!"

Science has been elevated, and
truth, wisdom, and good conduct have flown away.
Darkness has been established as the state of the mind.
Intoxicants, alcoholic beverages, love, the arts,
intoxicants, alcoholic beverages, the arts, love, dancing,
and business now rule,
and because of them man has become an animal.
Man has become the animal of all animals.
Because of that,
all the faces of men have become like those of
extremely dangerous animals.

O God, O my Father, You must come to us.
You must come to protect Your slaves and
grant us Your grace.
Stay in our hearts and grant us Your grace.
O my Father, You must come to us!
You must protect our hearts with Your grace,
so that satan and evil things do not enter us.
Watch over us and grant us Your grace.

Your kingdom, the *qalb* in the heart of man must remain.
It must remain a flower and praise You.
The *qalb-bū,* the *qalb-bū,*
the flower of the heart, the flower of the heart,
must not fade or wilt, it must not fade or wilt.
It must not be mesmerized.
You must pour the water of
Your compassionate love onto it.
You must water it so that it can bloom.
The *qalb-bū* needs Your grace in order to bloom.

O my Father, You must come to us.
You have to protect the flower of our heart
with Your grace.
We need Your blessing,
so that we may rest within You and commune with You.
O my Primal Father, You must come to us.
You must protect and give Your grace to Your slaves,
to all Your slaves.
Please protect them and give them Your grace.
Please protect them and give them Your grace.

Please protect them and give them Your grace.
Please protect them with compassionate love
and give them Your grace.
O Great Father, Allāhu.
O God, You are everything,
everything is You.
You are that fruit of the heart, and You must come to us.
You must come to protect us with Your grace.
*Āmīn. Āmīn.*
Yā Rabbal-ʿālamīn.
May it be so. May it be so.
O Creator of All the Universes.

# His Slave

*Tuesday, June 1, 1976, A.M.*

I AM ONE of the creations in God's creation,
I am one of the creations in God's creation,
a creation who is a slave,
a creation who is His slave.

I have come here for
service and duty,
compassion and love —
my duty is love.

I have come here to act with
the qualities that are complete.
I am one of the creations
created to act with
the qualities that are complete.

I am one of the creations who is a slave to God,
a slave, a poor creation,
a slave, a poor creation,
the lowest one, a creation who is a slave,
the lowest one, a creation who is a slave to all lives.

A small slave to all the creations,
a small slave to all the creations,
dust for the dust,
an ant for the ants,
an ant for the ants,
an atom for the atoms,
an atom for the atoms,
formed as a creation who is a slave.

I am one of the creations in the creation of God,
a creation who is a slave
to His servants, to those who love Him.
I am a creation
for His servants, for those who love Him,
a creation who serves them as a slave,
a creation who serves them as a slave.

I have come to give compassion, kindness, patience,
love, wisdom, and comfort to the poor,
as a creation who is a slave,
a creation who is a slave.

In the jungles and the cities,
in the oceans and the lands,
in the jungles and the cities,
in the oceans and the lands,
for the people, for the animals, and for the birds,
I am a creation created as a slave
who has come here to reveal and to nurture
the heart's witness, justice, and compassionate love,
the heart's witness, justice, and compassionate love.

I am the least of all lives.
I am the least of all lives,
a slave doing duty,
a slave doing duty,
a creation created by God.
I have been formed as a creation in God's creation
to perform the duty of a slave.

I am a creation
without jungle, city, town, or name,
without jungle, city, town, or name,
a creation without anything,
a creation without anything—
the poorest of slaves,
performing service and duty,
the poorest of slaves,
performing service and duty
as the heart's witness to God's love—
a slave imparting His grace,
a slave illustrating and imparting wisdom.

*Hi.*

**Dr. Markar:**[1] Now you know who he is!

---

1. Dr. Markar was one of Bawa Muhaiyaddeen's ☺ translators.

# The Good Day

*Thursday, August 4, 1977, 8:50 A.M.*

WHEN WILL THE GOOD day come,
the day that will be a good day for us?
When will the good day
of the resonance of the Grace of Allāhu come?
That day will be a good day for us.
When will the Grace that is Allāhu resonate?
That day will be a good day for everyone,
a good day for us.

When the *qalb*, the innermost heart,
is filled with justice
and truth dawns there,
when the *qalb* is filled with justice,
when the path that is truth appears,
the state of human justice will arise, and
a human being will live as a human being.
That will be a good day.
When that day comes to us,
it will be a good day for us.

115

Day and night the blessings of Ādi Rahmān[1]
who rules us,
day and night the blessings of Ādi Rahmān
who rules us,
will leap from heart to heart,
melt there and beat
between one human being and another.
When will that day come to us?
That day will be a good day for us.

When we live with justice,
the state of conscience,
melting compassion, patience, tolerance,
good conduct on the path of truth, and
when we live filled with goodness,
that day will be a good day for us.
That day will be a good day for us.
When will that day come?
When will that day come?

That day will be a good day
for mankind and for us.
It will be a day of exaltedness in our lives.
That day will occur on the day
we realize truth in a state of silence.
That will be an exalted day in our lives.
We will be aware of truth,
and we will walk on the good path.
That day will be a good day for us.

---

1. Ādi Rahmān (Tamil & Arabic n.) God, the Most Compassionate

The hearts of all mankind will resonate.
The bliss of grace will shine from their *qalbs.*
Justice and exaltedness will overflow from them.
They will live eternal lives of absolute integrity.
That day will be a good day for us.
That day will be a good day for us.
When will that day come to the world?
To everyone?
To all lives?
To those who have been born as human beings?

That will be an exalted day,
a good day.
That will be a good day for us.
That will be a good day in our lives.
Race, religion, and separation will be destroyed.
The peaceful qualities of truth and
justice will live among us.
Compassion for other lives will be most exalted.
Truth, justice, integrity, patience, compassion, love, and
*al-hamdu lillāh,* giving all praise to God,
will be most loved.

The day that mankind achieves that state
will be a good day for us.
That day will be the day the entire world will praise.
That day will be the day the state
of He who is One will be established.
That day will be the day He will stay with us.
That day will be the day He will rule.
That day will be the day of the praise known as *al-hamd.*

When will that day come?
That day will be a good day for us.
That day will be a good day for us.
On that day the state of
the just Rahmān will overflow from us,
compassion will arise from us, and
the divine Grace of our Creator
will descend into the *dunyā,* the world.

The heart will love this.
The *qalb* will love this.
The day that this occurs
in the life of man will be an exalted day.
That day will be a good day.
That will be a good day for us.
When will that day come?
That day will be an exalted, good day for us.

That will be the target and the arrow.
That will be the grace and the treasure.
That will be God and man.
The day they live as one
will be a good day.
The day they live as one
will be a good day.
When will that day come?

That day will be a good day for us
and for all lives.
That day will be a good day for all lives.

That will be the place
in which the sound will resonate.
That will be the grace
that will dispel our sins.
That will be the place
in which the sound will resonate.
That will be the grace
that will dispel our sins.
That will be the wisdom that destroys
the hypnotic delusion of the intellect.
The day that mankind
searches for this blessing and reaches it
will be a good day for mankind.
That day will be a good day for mankind.

When will that day come?
That day will be a good day for all lives.
It will be a day of service to God.
It will be a day the heart will be resonant
and attain grace.
It will be the day all lives attain peace.
That day will be the day all lives attain peace —
the day of service to God;
the day of service to the people;
the dawning of the day
of the crown of God in the kingdom of God.

When will that day come?
When will that day come?
That day will be a good day for us.

That will be an exalted day
when man lives amidst all lives;
the day of service to God;
the day of service to the people;
the day of dispensing justice
in a state of silence.
When will that day come?
When will that day come?
That day will be an exalted day for all lives.
What day will that come into being?
In death and in birth,
that day will be the exalted day
that belongs to Him.

# Life Is a Dream

*Thursday, October 13, 1977, 8:10 A.M.*

WHEN YOU SING a song, it has to come from God. The song has to come from God. It should not come from a book. It has to come from God. It has to come when you are totally absorbed in God.

This world is false; it is just a dream. This world is just a dream. Everything you see turns into a dream as soon as you are done looking at it. The world is just a series of scenes. It is composed of scenes, and each person is an actor. It is composed of scenes that are being acted over and over again.

*[Bawa Muhaiyaddeen ☺ sings:]*

God, the One alone,
God, the One alone
writes all the scenes.
God, the One alone
writes all the scenes.
His creations look at them and are overjoyed.
His creations look at them and are overjoyed.

Everything is mesmerizing.
Everything is mesmerizing.
Everything is trouble.
Everything is happy.
Everything is sad.

All the creations that believe in God,
act accordingly;
all the human beings that believe in God, believe in God,
act accordingly and
know that everything they see is a dream.
They know that everything they see is a dream.

If they analyze it, think of it with wisdom,
and look at it,
they see that life is just an empty dream.
They see that life is just an empty dream.

If human beings look at God's divine arts with love,
those [divine arts] will be the scenes of life,
the backdrops, the scenes
in front of which each person acts,
in front of which each person acts.

This is a stage,
and man is the actor.
This is a stage
for the drama of man's thoughts,
for the drama of man's thoughts.

For each person, for each person,
God writes and paints the scenes,
the backdrop for the drama.
These arts are kept within man's thoughts.
These arts are kept within man's thoughts.
They take form in the love within his mind,
and become dreams within his thoughts.
Man's life ends in acting.
This is the life of man.

If man realizes this within himself,
if man realizes and sees what is within,
he will see everything that was staged and written.
He will see all the lines of the story.
He will see all the lines of the story.
He will see that story as
the dream of his life,
the dream of his life,
the dream of his life.

Who knows what will happen tomorrow at
the end of the drama of the life in which he acts,
at the end of the drama of the life in which he acts?
Who knows what will happen tomorrow?
Who knows the acts that will take place tomorrow?
What will happen if he leaves this state of the "I?"
What will happen if he leaves this state of the "I?"

If he does not know his state or his end,
if he does not know his state or his end, or

the agreement [he made with God] about his life,
all his searching,
all his highs, all his lows,
all his acts,
all his drama, his dancing, his praising,
all his lines, and all his arts
will end as a useless dream.
They will end as a useless dream.

If man realizes this,
if he knows this with wisdom,
if he realizes this,
he will know that it is not real.
There will be no truth in this drama at all.

There is that One Light in *awwal*,
the beginning, the time of creation.
There is wisdom in this world.
There is clarity in his body.
He is resplendent beauty;
in *ākhirah*, in the world of God,
he is resplendent beauty.
In *ākhirah*, in the world of God,
he will become the beauty of God.

The agreement for the desires of
one who acts without knowing this
will end as a dream.
If man knows this, if man knows this,
and if he knows God,

if he receives this as Light,
the day that he understands will be grace.
The day that he understands will be grace.

O humankind,
if you look deeply with the heart at this birth,
if you realize the shining wisdom within it,
there will be no end to your life.
That state will shine as the Light
within the heart of your life.
It will resonate as the Light of God.
There will be no this world or next world for you,
there will be no this world or next world for you.
You will become God's open space of grace,
you will become God's open space of grace.

O humankind, come here.
Please realize this deeply and search for wisdom.
Immediately realize and look at this.
Study and realize this impermanent body.
Look at the shape of the muscles in the body; study them.
The body that is connected to karma is
a seed that came here for a certain time.
Its state was formed in sin.
It is a cage in which ten beings dwell.
It is a cage in which ten beings dwell.

It will reveal the seasons, the hours, and the minutes.
And in the end it will fall into the hands of
the Angel of Death.

It will reveal the end to the seasons,
the hours, and the minutes.
And in the end it will fall into the hands of
the Angel of Death.
Tomorrow it will go forth on a path,
unable to cross the bridge over hell.
It will proceed on the path to a desolate hell.
It will proceed on the path to a desolate hell.

O humankind, come here.
See with realized wisdom.
Recite your story quickly.
Look correctly at this impermanent body.
Look at the five and the six treasures within it.
If you analyze and realize what they are,
they will dawn as one Treasure—look at it.

If you look at it and know it well,
you will recite that there is only one God and
nothing else.
You will recite and say that
there is nothing other than God.
There will be no wife, child, livestock, or house.
You will not look for an attachment to a cow or a calf.

House and property are a cage.
Anything like this that you think of and intend to own
is an aspiration on the dark path.
It is a cage of the dark path.
It is a cage of the dark path.

Realize this with wisdom and look at it.
When the fanaticism, arrogance, and karma
are destroyed,
this will be a good house.
When the fanaticism, arrogance, and karma
are destroyed,
this will be a good house.

If you realize this within your heart, and look,
you will find the grace of the three worlds.
If you realize and look at what is within,
you will see the Light that has no form at all.
You will see the Light that has no form at all.

O humankind, come here.
Recite of the path in silence.
Realize this truth and look,
realize your truth and look.
The state of peace will come; look at
the state of established peace.
Search for the grace of God that exists peacefully,
search for the grace of God that exists peacefully.

Jeweled lights of my eyes, come here.
Place your intention upon the divine Grace of your Creator.
Read what is within your body, and look at it.
It is telling you that all the days of your life are false,
look.
It is telling you that all the days of your life are false,
look.

This musical story is a dream.
All the words you speak,
all the words you speak are dreams.
Everything that you do not realize within is wasted.
If you look at it closely, you will know.
If you look at it closely, you will know.

O humankind, come here.
Look at the One who is King of all the heavenly realms.
Look at this birth,
look at this birth.
Pray,
and think of the reason you have come here.
There is a great story within your body.
Your life is just a dream of your heart.
Your arrival is a great history.
Look at what is within you and read it.
Look at what is within you and read it.

There is a cage of bliss made of twenty-eight letters.
They shine as a great Qur'ān,
the letters shine as a great Qur'ān.
This is a cage made of *hikmat,* the secrets of wisdom,
this mysterious Qur'ān,
this mysterious Qur'ān from
the King of all the heavenly worlds.

Nothing can ever destroy this treasure.
If you look into this deeply with wisdom,

at the beautiful *surahs*
of the Qur'ān which shine there,
if you look at the *Sūrah* of *Al-hamd*[1] and recite it,
if you know that *surah,*
what destruction can there ever be for you?
If you look at that *surah,*
what destruction can there ever be for you?

God who is immeasurable Grace will come.
He will exist belonging equally to everyone.
He will shine everywhere.
He will be the Rahmān,
the most Compassionate One,
belonging equally to everyone.
He will belong equally to everyone as the Rahmān,
the most Compassionate One.
Your entire heart will be completely full.
He will give you the one Resonance of Allāhu,
and Allāhu will resonate and shine and exist there.
Allāhu will resonate
and shine and exist there.
The *"hu"* of illAllāhu will resonate, resonate,
resplend, and come to shine.
It will come to shine and resplend.

---

1. *Sūrah* of *Al-hamd* (Arabic n.) the Chapter of Praise, the *Sūratul-Fātihah,* the opening chapter of the Qur'ān

The *sallAllāhu* of the *salawāt*[2]
is the resonance of the
*kalimah*[3] of the form of peace.
This is the explanation of the twenty-four letters,
given by wisdom.
Your soul will become resonant as the twenty-fifth.

The *Sūratul-Fātihah* will shine
within you there as His grace.
It will shine as the source,
it will shine as the source of the *dhāt*, the grace;
it will shine as the source.
It will shine as the *dhāt*, the grace of God, the Creator.

This is the grace of God's explanation,
the grace of God's explanation,
for this world and for the hereafter.[4]

If you resonate with this *salawāt,*
if you bring the *kalimah* of peace up and down, and
if you look into your body,
nothing will be there, oh,

---

2. *sallAllāhu* of the *salawāt* (Arabic phrase) Prayers to God asking for blessings for the Prophet ☉, for the believers, and for everyone. *SallAllāhu 'alā Muhammad; sallAllāhu 'alaihi wa sallam.* May Allāh bless Muhammad; may Allāh bless him and grant him eternal peace. *SallAllāhu 'alā Muhammad; yā Rabbi salli 'alaihi wa sallim.* May Allāh bless Muhammad; O my Lord bless him and grant him peace.
3. *kalimah* (Arabic n.) *La ilāha illAllāhu:* There is nothing other than You, O God. Only You are Allāh.
4. *inmay* (n.) this life, the here; *marumay* (n.) the hereafter

nothing will be there other than the one God!
Look at Him.

The entire world of pure souls will shine in your heart.
Look at it.
The entire world of pure souls will shine in your heart.
Look at it.
The eight heavens will shine there.
The seven hells will also be there.
The Nabī ☙, the Prophet of the fragrance of
blossoming grace will shine there.
The Nabī ☙, the Prophet of the fragrance of
blossoming grace will shine there.

Feeling, awareness, intellect, assessment,
subtle wisdom, divine analytic wisdom, and
the resplendence of divine luminous wisdom
will be within you.
The Master of Birth and Death will be there.
If you realize this with wisdom and look at it,
you will understand.
The story of the soul will shine everywhere.
The story of the soul will shine everywhere.

If you know this fundamental story,
if you realize the clarity of the creation of God,
if you understand all of His artwork,
if you realize this in your heart,
what more can you ever want?

If you realize the *qalb* which is known as your heart,
if you understand all of these things,
if you distinguish between good actions and bad actions,
if you look at what is good and study it,
if you look at what is good and study it,
there will be only one thing in your heart.
There will be only one thing in your heart.
You will see nothing else there,
you will see nothing else on this day.

Peace and contentment will shine.
That universe will resonate as one.
The world of pure souls will resplend.
*Awwal* and *ākhirah* will be resplendent everywhere.
The Light of that state is the grace that fills the heart.
See the resonance of illAllāhu call to you.
See it resonating and vibrating
throughout your whole body.

You need peace for the state of tranquility.
You need certitude for the state of *īmān,*
the state of absolute faith in God.
You need truth to see He who is One.
You need wisdom to find Him and to catch Him.
You have to chase away and get rid of ignorance
to understand the Nūr, the Light of true wisdom.
The helpful story of the One above is shining within you,
look.

If you see this state,
what will you see as unhappiness in this world?
What unhappiness will you ever have in this world?
The state that will exist for you
in the world of God,
the world of *awwal* and this *dunyā;*
the state in which you exist
will be with God.

The state in which you dwell will be the state of heaven.
The state in which you exist will be God's state.
The state in which you exist will be God's state.
Where you live will be heaven.
Everywhere you dwell will be the kingdom of God.
Here and there,
that will be the state of He who is One.
Here and there,
with the help of He who is One,
you will rule here and everywhere,
you will rule here and everywhere.

Look at this with expanding wisdom.
Search for the most exalted grace-awakened wisdom.
With the certitude of *īmān,*
establish the intention
to merge with the one God, illAllāhu,
to merge with the one God, illAllāhu.
Recite the *salām* and the *salawāt.*
Join with the one Treasure that is alone.

O humankind,
the history of your birth
is your home, your house in *ākhirah,* your heaven.
That is your own home,
your very own home.
That is the house of the beauty and the grace of your life.
That is the state He will give you.
Realize this and look at it.
Merge with the path on which you can analyze this.

The birth that you see,
the birth that you look at,
the form of this cage of the body,
is a form of ignorance
for all the songs that you have sung,
for all the places in which you have studied.
This house of history to which you have come
is a rented house.
This is just a rented house.

This is just a form
made of skin and bones and
muscles and blood and flesh and
many colors, many hues, many sections, many languages.
This house is full of those things,
this house of skin and flesh.
You are just renting it.
You have come here to learn in it.
Look at it, be clear about it, and study.

There are twelve parts to its history.
If you study them, you will understand.
If you pass the test,
then you can happily go to your Father.
He will give you a job and a house,
a career and a place in which to live.
He will give them to you there.
In truth, He will give you that place, that title,
that grace, that heaven.
He will give them to you as your own.
He will give you a title.
That is truly your own house.

Look at your Father.
He will belong to you.

You have come here only to study for that test.
You have come here to understand the arts that God,
your Father, has created:
the arts and sciences, the songs, the games,
the sun and the moon and the stars,
the earth, the sky, the world, and the underworlds,
and many other creations,
the trees and many creations,
the colors, the hues, the languages, the sounds,
the tones, the tunes, the tones, the tunes.
Understand them and look at them,
pray, and praise your Father.

The story you have come here to see and to study is that
of the trees, the bushes, the little flowers, their sweetness,
their sweetness, their fragrances,
the birds and the animals, all of them.

After you have finished looking at them,
after you become clear,
after you leave this dream world,
after you leave this cage full of memories,
after you leave the enchantment of this house of desire,
after you leave this house that is a place of ignorance,
an eternity will exist for you with your Father,
an eternity will exist for you with your Father.

Then you can quickly go into your home and stay there.
Then your story will belong to you.
Then your life will exist
without any bonds or attachments.
Then if you reach that state of maturity,
if you destroy the main root of
those sins and that karma—
the sins, the arrogance, the illusion,
the enchantments of the darkness of ignorance—
God alone will be your Father.
There will be no other help for you here.

If you pray, and realize it within,
what destruction can there be for you in this world?
What sorrow can there be for you in this world?
What evil can there be for you in this world?

What karma can there be for you in this world?
What sin can there be for you in this world?
If you realize the truth, what else is there?
There will be no friend for you other than the one God.
Please realize this and look at it with wisdom.

My beloved children,
before this maya which is karma reaches its final state,
before the world of dreams ends,
before the world of dreams ends,
before you know this and see this,
it will appear and stand before you as bliss.
But after you look at it with wisdom,
your dream life will end,
your dream life will end.

You must realize this deeply and look at it.
You must realize the truth and study it.
You must quickly know this and look at it.
Then you will know all your faults in the story.
You must quickly know this and look at it.
Then you will know all your faults in the story.

You must dispel all your faults
without being attached to them.
You must chase away all your sins.
You must walk on the path and join with the Truth.
You must see the one God and obtain His help.
You must follow Him with love.

When you find your true life,
what sorrow can there be for you in this world?
What happiness can there be for you in this world?
What birth can there be for you in this world?
There will be nothing here except the dream.
There will be nothing.
It will only be a dream.
God alone will be real to you.
Know this and realize this,
my children who have been born with me,
children, my very own children.

# Who Belongs to Us in the World?

*Wednesday, November 23, 1977, 3:45 P.M.*

WHO BELONGS TO ANYONE in the world?
Who belongs to us in this world?
Who belongs to whom in this world?
Who belongs to anyone in this world?
Who belongs to anyone in this world?
Who was born with us?
What are the diseases that will kill us?
Who was born with us?
Who will go with us?

Who came with us as the disease that will kill us,
as the disease that will kill us?
Who came with us?
Who was born with us?
Who will go with us?
Who will cleave to us like the disease born with us,
the disease that will kill us?
Who is as connected to us as the disease born with us,
the disease that will kill us?
Who belongs to whom?
Who belongs to whom in the world?

Who belongs to anyone in this world?
Who will go with us when we go tomorrow?
Who will go with us when we go tomorrow?
Who will take a share of our illnesses,
our suffering, our diseases?
Who will take a share of our illnesses,
our diseases, our suffering?

Who will take a share
of our pain, of the misery of our mind,
of our agreement with God,
of our judgment,
of our dual state of good and evil,
in the grave,
during the questioning,
on the Day of Judgment?
Who will take a share
of the punishment, or
of our happiness?
Who will share this with us?

Who, who, who was born with us?
Who is He?
Who, who, who is the One born with us?
Who will go with us?
Who will share our illnesses, diseases, and suffering?
The disease that will kill us was born with us.
The disease that will kill us was born with us;
it will stay with us until it kills us in the end,
it will stay with us until it kills us in the end.

What is the purpose of all this suffering,
all this misery, all this pain?
What is the purpose of this illness?
In this state, who was born with us in the world?
Who will go with us?
Who will share our suffering?
O, who, who is He?
Who is He in the world?
Who is the One that belongs to us in this world?
Who belongs to us?

The people of the world are all
like the shade of a deadwood tree,
like the shade of a deadwood tree.
The people of the world all attend to their own states,
alone, alone.
They live their lives in selfishness.
Just as the shadow follows the sun, circling
all four compass points,
they change according to the times.
They change their lives.
They change alliances.
They change attachments.
They live their lives depending on shadows.
Their lives are written on water.
They come back, changed, turned around.

Who belongs to whom in the world?
Who was born with us?
Who will go with us?

Who will share
our illnesses, our diseases, our suffering,
our heights, and our depths?
Who will share this with us?
Who belongs to whom in this world?

Morning time, afternoon time, evening time, night time—
see how the times change,
see how the times change.
See how our development will change similarly
in this birth.
See how the state of our development will change
during these four times,
the way that our life changes during that development,
the way that our life changes during that development.
All those attached to the connection of earth, fire,
water, air, and ether,
all the people who appear, all the lives, all the forms,
all the self-images,
their belongings, their attachments, and their relatives
will change.
They will all change.
They will all change.

When will that change take place?
The four times will change,
just as the four seasons change.
That can be understood anywhere in the world.
Everyone knows this.
Because of this,

who belongs to whom in the world?
Who belongs to anyone in this world?
Who was born with us?
Who will go with us?
Who will share
our suffering, our illness, our hunger,
our old age, and our death?
Who will take a share of it?
Who will take a share of our illnesses?

You have created this dream-world as a thought,
and the demons of the mind
will play with desire tomorrow,
the demons of the mind will play with desire tomorrow.
They will play primarily
with their blood ties.
You think of them,
but all your thoughts are dreams.
Your thoughts are all dreams.
The thoughts of your mind are all dreams;
all your desires are the darkness.

Do not believe in the dreams that you see in the darkness,
do not live mesmerized by them.
Do not think it is life.
Do not think that the world is life.
Do not believe that they are your own
blood ties, relatives, and attachments.
Do not believe that they are your own
blood ties, relatives, and attachments.

Do not favor those who have no help as your helpers.
Do not favor those who have no help as your helpers.

This is a bitter illness.
This is a bitter illness in life.
Do not believe that it will make you healthy.
This is a bitter illness.
Do not believe that it will make you healthy.
This is the disease that will kill you.
This is the disease that was born with us,
the disease that is tormenting us,
the disease that is chasing us off the path,
the disease that will guide us to the jungle,
the disease that will take us into karma,
the disease that will pour us into many rebirths,
the disease of bile,
the disease of insanity,
the disease of bile,
the disease of insanity,
the disease of ancestry,
the disease of hysteria.
This is hysteria—
history is hysteria, the hysteria of history.
If you believe in the disease of history,
you will not believe the truth.

Who was born with you?
Who came with you?
Who lives with you?
Do not depend upon anyone who lives with you.

There is no one who will take a share
of your illnesses and diseases.
No one will go with you.
No one will gather up your sorrow.
No one will take a share of
your suffering, your illness, your old age, or your death.

O humankind!
The disease that will kill you was born with you.
It is the painful, agonizing disease that is in
our qualities, our desires, and our minds.
It is the disease of attachment
that approaches us as a relative.
It is the disease that gathers up many sins.
It is the disease that points us towards many, many rebirths.
It is the disease that subjects us to horrible sins.
It is the disease that dwells intermingled
in the center of our eyes, our mind, and our desire.

O humankind!
Please look deeply into this.
Know this quickly and run.
Who belongs to whom?
Who was born with you?
Who was born with you?
Who was born with you in this world?
Who came with you?
Who will share
in your happiness and in your sadness,

in your hunger and in your illness,
in your disease and in your death?
Who will protect you?

O humankind!
Please look at this quickly.
Think of it and run away.
Who belongs to whom?
Who belongs to whom in this world?

There is something intermingled with your life.
There is a Grace intermingled with your body.
Even if your mother and father forget you,
there is that One Thing that is God who
will never forget you, and
who will protect you.

There is that One Thing intermingled
in the earth, in the sky, and in you.
There is that One Thing intermingled
in love, in grace, and in wisdom.
There is that One Thing dwelling
in your soul, in your life, and in your being.
There is that One Thing which dwells
in the truth within you.
There is that One Thing which dwells
as Reality within reality within you,
and that provides for you.

There is that One Thing which is intermingled
as Love within love.
There is that One Thing which dwells
as the Soul within the soul.
There is that One Thing which dwells
as the Soul within the soul.
There is that One Thing which is intermingled with you
now and forever.
There is that One Thing which will share in all the dangers.
There is that One Thing which will protect you in
happiness and sadness.
There is that One Thing which will feed you and
protect you in hunger and illness.
There is that One Thing which will be the Watcher
in the darkness and in the daylight.
There is that One Thing which will be the Watcher
living within you,
while you walk and while you are still.

In every way,
He is God who dwells with us and who protects us.
Other than God,
who belongs to us?
Other than God,
who belongs to us?
Who belongs to us other than God who created us?
Who protects us?
He is with us here, there, and everywhere.
Here, there, everywhere!

In the embryo, in the form,
in food, in water,
in hunger, in illness, in old age,
in death, in Judgment,
in the *awwal,* in the *ākhirah,*
He is God who is with you.
He is God who protects you.
He is God who watches you.
He is God who protects you in so many ways
and who takes you to the shore.
Other than that,
who is with you in the world?

He is God, exalted in all three worlds.
He is God who is the Light in the center of your eyes.
He is God who perceives
the fragrance that comes to the nose.
He is God who knows the taste in the tongue.
He is God who hears the sounds that come to the ears.
He is God who speaks as the Light within wisdom.
He is God who reveals the Compassion within love.
He is God who lives in the heart.
He is God, our Creator, our divine God.

Other than that,
who belongs to us?
Other than that,
who will come with us in the world?
Other than that,
who will help us in this world?

Realize this and look at it.
Believe that there is no help other than this
and recite:
There is no one other than God.
No one other than God will help us.
No one in this world is greater than God.
There is no other God anywhere that protects us.

What else is there?
What else belongs to us?
What else is there for us in the world or anywhere else?
What else is there?

# Allāh, in the World, You Are a Pearl

*Sunday, February 12, 1978, 10:30 P.M.*

Allāh,
in *'ālamul-arwāh,*
in the world of pure souls,
You are a Germinating Seed.

Allāh, in the world,
You are a Pearl.
Allāh, in the world,
You are a Pearl.

To everything in the world of pure souls,
You are a Germinating Seed of Bliss.

To the *qalb,*
You are a Light
that has come
as the explanation of *gnānam,*
as the blissful Germinating Seed of Divine Wisdom.

Allāh, to the *qalb,*
You are a Pearl.

To everything in the world of pure souls,
You are a Germinating Seed.

To the *qalb*, You are Beauty.
O Creator,
You are a Germinating Seed in the blissful *qalb*.

To honesty, You are a Light.
For the attainment of peace in the *qalb*,
You are the Grace of Divine Wisdom.

For this world and the next world,
You are the Conclusion.
For this world and the next world,
You are the Limit, the Conclusion.

For *hayāh*, for life,
for attaining absolute and eternal liberation,
You are a Feast for the *qalb*.

You came into *gnānam* and were born there.
You came to the place in which the *qalb* exists,
and You dwelled there.
You melted and dissolved into wisdom.
You were born in the heart of *īmān*.

To the skies and to the earth,
You are a Medicine.

To the creations of all kinds,
You are a Father.
To all lives,
You are a Father.

You are the One who gives food
to all lives.
You are the One who gives food
to all lives,
the Beautiful One who serves them.

You are the King who rules
the microcosm and the macrocosm.

You are the blissful Pearl of Divine Wisdom
that comes into the heart and resplends there.

For this world and the next world,
You are the blissful Conclusion.

You are a Medicine
that grants peace in this life, in *hayāh,*
a Feast of Bliss that grants peace,
a Treasure of Bliss
that reveals tranquility within my *qalb.*

If You would come here now,
that would be an eternal victory.

If my heart would resonate,
that would be the happiness of my life.

If my *qalb* would blossom as a flower,
You would be the fragrance there.

If I intermingled with You,
that would be the state of Light.

Within thought,
You are the blissful One.

Within wisdom,
You are the resonant One.

Within love,
You are the intermingled One.

Within the *āmīn*,[1]
You are the One who says the *salām*.[2]

Within justice,
You are the One who rules.

You are the One who leads
a life of peace,
the Father who is the Creator,

---

1. *āmīn* (Arabic n.) may it be so, amen
2. *salām* (Arabic n.) the greeting of peace

the Almighty One who dispels our karma,
the Lord who never forgets the truth,
the Father to all lives,
the Lord who is patient with our mistakes.

You are Khudā, the One who is God.
You are the One who accepts the responsibility
when the *āmīn* is said.

You are the One who recites
the *salām* and the *salawāt*
within the heart.

You are the Almighty One
who resonates alone.

You are the Allāhu who resonates and stands
within the resplendent word illAllāhu.

# Search for the Light

*Sunday, February 19, 1978, 10:00 A.M.*

So MUCH TIME has passed since we were conceived,
since the day we were conceived.
Our mind has not changed, it has not yet left us.
So many seasons have changed,
so many seasons have changed,
yet the mind of man has not changed for even one day.
The oceans have turned into lands and
the lands have turned into oceans;
jungles have turned into cities.
Many beings have changed.

Even though everything else is changing,
this mind of man has not changed for even one day.
Even though the whole world is turning upside down,
the mind that lives in the body of man never changes.
His thoughts and desires have not been dispelled.
He has not dispelled the hell in which he exists.
Even though so many yugas, so many eons,
have come and come and changed and gone,
the mind of man has not changed.
He has not dispelled his desire or his karma.

This birth is so rare.
His birth is such a wonder.
His life is just a splinter and
like a bubble in the water.
He lives his daily life;
his life is like a dream.
He thinks it has meaning.
His life is like a dream.
He thinks it has meaning.

He thinks he is carrying the world.
He grows himself by raising and eating many lives.
He is full of murders and sins.
He joyously thinks he is king of the whole world.
He has lost his own state.
He came into being as just an atom.
Man is the one who lives in that state —
he has not yet realized what his state is.
His life is like a dream.
He has not looked into and thought of the meaning.
His life is like a bubble in the water.
But he lives thinking he is going to be immortal.

Hey you, who have appeared in this mind of maya!
Try to realize your human birth.
How many births are you going to have?
How many tens of millions of births are you going to take?
Your life is a bubble in the water.
It is the state of your karma.
If you do not pull out

the states of arrogance, karma, and maya by the roots,
your life will be just a bubble in the water.
If you do not pull out
the states of arrogance, karma, and maya by the roots,
your life will be just a bubble in the water,
your life will be just a bubble in the water.

Think of your impermanent life —
your attempts to permanently rule the world are false,
your attempts to permanently rule the world are false.
You have a false body
established by earth, fire, water, air, and ether, the colors.
You just have that kind of form.
All your thoughts and ideas become dreams.
All your thoughts and ideas become dreams.

All that you do, all your thoughts are wasted.
If you do not pull out and uproot
the state of the karma of your birth,
it will become a bubble in the water.
Your life is like a dream.
You think you are immortal and that
you are not going to die in the end, but you will.
You eat by causing pain to other lives.
You live by killing those who have been born with you.
You will die carrying the earth.
You will whirl and spin and die in this hypnotic state.

Yet if you do realize this state,
how much happiness there will be in your birth.

If you realize the truth,
you will get such exalted titles and states in your life.
Look at and quickly realize this.
Search for your form
within the form of peacefulness and truth.
Try to purify your heart with the determination of *īmān,*
absolute faith.
Enter into the determination within determination,
and merge with the Light within that divine Light.
Three, *alif, lām,* and *mīm,*[1] will be there:
the Qutb ☺, the Rasūl ☺, and Allāh.
Your *ānmā,* your soul, will be there as well.
The *rūh,* the soul, will be a Light.

If you do not know this state,
your life will be as permanent as that of an ant.
You will die like a bubble in the water.
Your life will have no permanence—it will go;
it will perish.
Establish an eternal life
and look at your life.

Everything dies.
Other than God, everything dies.
That one Truth does not die.
That Light never disappears.
Allāh has no appearance.
Your soul, your *ānmā,* the *rūh,* never perishes.

---

1. *alif, lām,* and *mīm* (Arabic n.) Three letters of the Arabic alphabet. See Glossary.

If you are to have an indestructible life,
search for the Rabb, the Lord
who created and placed the indestructible life of
the *rūh* in your body.
Search for the Light that Allāh created and placed
within your body.
Intend to reach that Truth.
Love Allāh, be with Allāh, and join with Allāh.

Without this state,
you will be in hell for your birth and for your death.
You will be subject to birth and death.
Your life will be a dream.
Your births will never end;
you will be endlessly reborn.

O human beings,
look at this with wisdom.
Search for *adab*[2] and good conduct.
Search for *adab* and good conduct.
If you realize this state,
then Allāhu, illAllāhu will resonate.
Then illAllāhu will resonate.
Then *īmān* will shine within this resonance.
You will see three letters within this state:
The Qutb ☺, the Nūr Muhammad will be there as letters,
the Rabb will be a shining Light.

---

2. *adab* (Arabic n.) good manners, decency, courtesy, propriety, as exemplified in the life of Prophet Muhammad ☺

That is what will merge with you as your soul.
That Light will be a life without any death.
Life without death is life.
If you search for it,
you can live forever without change.
You can live merged with God.
Then you can live without this world or the hereafter.

If you do not reach this state,
your life will be like a bubble in the water.
The happiness in your life will be a dream.
Everything you set into motion will be
an act on this stage.
Everything you see and do and eat will be hell.

O humankind, look at this and realize this.
O humankind, look at this and realize this deeply.
Search for the Light that is your Khudā, your God.
Search for the Light that is your Khudā, your God.
You have to become the Light within the Light.

If you do not become this,
your life will be wasted.
All the time you spend in the world will be wasted.
All the time you spend in the world will be wasted.

# When You Pray and Your Heart Melts

*Thursday, February 23, 1978, 1:00 P.M.*

WHEN THE HEART melts,
when the heart melts,
God's glory will come to merge with us.
When the heart melts,
God's glory will come to merge with us.
When the heart melts within us,
God's glory will come to merge with us.
When love melts, when love melts within us,
God's love and grace will come to merge with us,
God's love and grace will come to merge with us.

When the heart melts,
Allāh's incomparable grace will come to merge with us.
When the heart melts,
Allāh's incomparable love will come to merge with us.
When the *qalb,* the heart, melts,
Allāh's own compassion will come to merge with us.
When our *qalbs* melt,
the compassionate Light of Allāh's Nūr will come to
merge with us.

When wisdom melts,
Allāh's love and refuge will come to merge with us.
When wisdom melts,
Allāh's grace and bliss will come to merge with us.
When *imān,* absolute faith, melts,
the ocean of compassion that is the Light in the heart
will come to merge with us,
the ocean of compassion that is Allāh's Light in the heart
will come to merge with us.

When determination, certitude, and *imān* are
established within us,
the Light known as Nūr Muhammad, that Light,
His grace, His qualities, His actions, His behavior, and
His perfect and pure completion
will come to merge with us.
They will come to merge with us.
In the darkness and in the daylight
God will enter into and comfort
those who correctly perform His prayer
that existed before and that will exist afterwards.

In the darkness and in the daylight
God will enter into and comfort
those who correctly perform His prayer
that existed before and that will exist afterwards.
In sleep and in wakefulness,
Allāh is the incomparable Ruler of Grace.

When you pray with a melting *qalb*,
Allāh will give you the grace to be one with Him.
Allāh will give you the grace to be one with Him.
When you forget yourself,
when you forget yourself,
when you exist worshipping God alone,
when you lose the earth,
Allāh will come in His state of silence.

When we lose our desire,
Allāh will give us the state in which He Himself exists.
Allāh will give us the state in which He Himself exists.
When the mind is controlled,
He will grant control of everything to one atom,
He will grant control of everything to one atom.
He will be the Atom within the atom.
You will merge with Him as One,
you will merge with Him as One.

When patience and tolerance come to you,
He will give you the grace to rule His kingdom
as your kingdom.
When *sabūr*, inner patience, and *shukūr*, contentment,
come to you,
when *sabūr* and *shukūr* come to you,
Allāh will bestow the scepter of His kingdom upon you.
When the certitude of *al-hamd*, praise to God,
comes to you,
when the certitude of *al-hamd* comes to you from Him,
He will give you the scepter of His justice.

It is to *insān* and God as one that
He will grant the grace to rule His kingdom.
He will make Allāh and His messenger
the Chieftain in His kingdom.
That One will be made the Chieftain of His kingdom.
He will belong equally to all people.
He will bring peace of mind, justice, and truth.
He will bring peace of mind, justice, and truth.
He will dwell hidden in all lives,
revealing the explanation.
Everything in *'ālamul-arwāh,*
the world of pure souls, and everywhere
will bow in obeisance to him.
*Insān* in this state
will be in a state of worship and love for God.

If he [man] walks in the world,
securing His qualities one by one,
he will become His messenger.
He will receive the state of His messenger.
He will be the Chieftain of that secret, silent kingdom.
If you realize this within the meaning,
if you hold on to this as your lifeline while you walk,
if you accept these actions to be rightfully yours,
what else will there be for you in the world?
What other than God will there be for you in this world?

If one who reaches this state becomes a human being,
he will be one without anyone else in this world.
He will accept no help other than His.

# Believe in God

*Sunday, February 26, 1978, 9:45 A.M.*

O HUMANKIND, look a little,
O humankind, look a little,
look at this world.
O humankind, look here, look deeply at the world.
O you who are wise among humankind,
come here, come here.
You who are wise, come here, come here.
Look at the world,
look deeply into all the visible things,
look into all the visible things.
Look into them, look into them deeply.

Every created thing has a beauty to the eyes.
Everything that has appeared is a wonder. But,
not everything you see is appropriate to *gnānam*,
to the state of *gnānam*, to wisdom.
Not all of it is appropriate for the meaning of wisdom.
It does not fit the truth.

Do not be subject to the state of hypnotic delusion in
which the entire world exists.
This world is all a hypnotic delusion.

Do not be in that state.
It is not suitable to wisdom.
Everything visible is a scene.
Everything you look at is a hypnotic delusion.
Everything you hear is the mind.
Everything you hear is the happiness and
the sadness of the mind.

Because of that, O wise ones, come here.
Look at the world.
Understand it deeply and listen.
Understand it deeply and listen.
Understand it deeply and listen.
Look at it with the wisdom of your birthright.
Everything visible,
everything you look at,
everything you enjoy,
everything you praise,
everything you laugh at,
everything that makes you happy—
look at what these things are.
Understand and look deeply to see of what use they are.

They will be the darkness that conceals you,
the darkness that conceals you.
They will all be the things that will destroy you.
They will all be the actions that will destroy you.
They will make you subject to the karmic births
of this world.
They will make you subject to the karmic births
in this world, to many rebirths.

Do not believe in this.
Pretend to believe in it and escape.
Pretend to believe in it and then escape.
Do not believe in it.
If you do believe in it,
danger will come to you,
and many evils will hurt you.
They will kill you.
They will destroy you.
They will subject you to a state of danger.

O humankind, come here.
Look at this world.
Look deeply into yourself and listen.
There is a story within your open heart.
Know all the meanings within it.
Listen to that [story],
listen to it.
Do that,
understand and see everything:
"That is happiness,
that is sadness,
that is what you like,
that is what you like!"
Understand everything you hear and look at it.

The things that speak to you,
the things that laugh with you,
the things that speak to you,
laugh with you and cry with you,

are the diseases that were born with you and
that will kill you.
Understand that they are all diseases born with you
that will kill you.
They will be your blood.
They will be your flesh.
They will be your bones.
They will be your skin, flesh, bones, and muscles.
They will be your body.

Within it will be colors, hues, religions,
and ethnic groups in many millions of forms.
There will be scriptures, philosophies, knowledge,
titles, and honors.
There will be lust, gold, treasures,
gold, treasures, torpor, and joy.
There will be ties to blood, attachments,
relatives, belongings, and kinship.
They will take many tens of millions of forms.
They will be the friends born with you.

They will show you love and affection.
They will be loving and supportive.
Those things will say, "We will die with you."
Those things will say, "We will die with you."
They will give you peace and speak to you.
They will give you peace and speak to you.
But after you die, they will remain in the earth.
Those five will intermingle with the earth,
desert you, and leave you.

Understand and see that they are in a state of deceiving you.
Even though they are with you,
if you look into this deeply with wisdom,
you will know.
If you look into this deeply with wisdom,
you will know.
You will be clear about yourself.
You will know your body,
and you will know all your relatives and relationships.

Because of that, O humankind, come here.
Look at the world.
Open yourselves and look.
Open your hearts, speak there,
and know what all those friends within you
are asking for.

Pretend to believe in all that they say.
When you listen, pretend to believe what they say.
Do not believe them.
Pretend to believe them,
but do not listen to them, do not believe what they say
or do what they say.
If you believe them,
that will become a state of danger for you.

O humankind, that will become a state of danger for you.
It will subject you to many rebirths,
and in the end it will take you to the state of hell,
in the end it will take you to the state of hell.

O humankind, come here.
Look at the world.
Know yourself and recite.
Open your heart and look.
Listen to the story being told within your body.
Do not believe that these things are your friends.
Do not believe that these things are your friends.
Do not shout that these things will stay with you.
Do not believe in these relatives and relationships,
this "I" and this "mine."

Pretend to believe in them,
but do not believe in them.
Pretend to believe in them,
but do not believe in them.
O humankind, do not believe in them.

Everything visible is a scene.
Everything you see,
everything that makes you happy is a hypnotic delusion.
Everything you eat is hell.
Everything you see is seen
through the shadow of the hypnotic delusion of desire.
Those things will become the shadow of your desire.
Everything you see becomes a dream.

In the end, your state will be that of
embryos in many forms,
the embryos of many forms.
You will be subject to many rebirths.

It will be a state that will take you apart and
put you together again.

Because of that, O humankind, come here.
Look at the world.
Open yourself and look within.
Look with wisdom.
When you speak with these things,
when you listen, pretend to believe
all that you hear,
all that you hear,
all that you say to them and
all that they say to you,
but do not believe them.
Do not believe them.
Do not believe them.
Do not believe them.

O humankind, come here.
Look at yourselves.
Open your hearts and go gently within.
Come.
The *Qalb* within the *qalb,*
the Wisdom within wisdom,
the Light within Light,
the Life within life,
the Completion within completion,
the Completion within completion,
the state of Mystery,
the one Treasure that is a Mystery,

the Grace that is wise,
that complete Treasure that is bliss is Allāhu,
it is the Power known as Allāhu.

Know this and look at this.
Believe in That.
Deeply believe in That.
Do not ever pretend to believe in That.
Do not ever pretend to believe in That.
Determinedly believe in That.
Believe in that Treasure.
Believe in That.

Do not ever just pretend to believe in That.
Do not ever pretend to believe in That in the world.
If you pretend to believe in That,
you will be in more danger than
the danger we spoke of before.
You will be in more danger than
the danger we spoke of before.
That will be a state that will shake apart your wisdom.
That will be a state that will bring many rebirths to
your life.
That will be the state of deceiving Him, deceiving God
who is the One in the Heart within the heart,
the One who is God.

You will be a thief to all lives.
You will be a criminal.
You will be an enemy to God,

the jeweled Light within my eyes.
You will be an enemy to God,
the jeweled Light within my eyes.

O humankind, come here.
Look at yourselves.
Open your *qalbs* and recite within.
Inside are the seventy thousand veils.
Tear those veils apart and go beyond them.
Look inside and speak to the One who is there alone.
He will merge with you and you will be His friend.
Do not ever deceive Him.
Do not ever pretend to believe in Him.
Truly believe in Him.
Believe in Him.
Believe in Him.

Do not ever just pretend to believe in Him.
Do not ever pretend to believe in Him in the world.
Do not ever pretend to believe in Him in the world.

He is the One in all lives.
He is in the center of the light within the eyes.
He is the One within the heart who sees you.
He is the Sound within the sound.
He is the One intermingled with the fragrance within
the fragrance in your nose.
He is the Taste within the taste in the tongue.
He is the Mighty One in the open heart who knows.

He is the One who knows the state of
the blood and the skin.
He is the One who is complete in all lives, and
who dwells in them.

He is the Witness who will speak first.
He is the One who knows and sees all lives.
He exists in all lives as an Atomless Being.
There is nothing that would move in any life without Him,
He is such a Being.
He is omnipresent in all lives.
Without Him,
without Him,
no life would ever move.
He is the One who makes it all move.
He is the Ruler of Grace.
He is the most loving One.
He is the unfathomable Ruler of Grace.
He is incomparable Love.
He is the One who is the undiminishing wealth.
He is God who is known as Khudā.

He is the One who is complete everywhere,
intermingled in earth, in sky, everywhere.
He is the One who knows Himself and
all the invisible beings.
He is intermingled in and dwells in all lives.
He resonates alone as illAllāhu.
He is the Almighty One.

The One who knows you will know everything.
He will ask the questions regarding good and evil.
He will give food day and night.
He is the original One who carries us
in the darkness and in the daylight.
He is the blissful, mysterious One, the formless One,
the mysterious One, the formless One,
the One who cannot be controlled by anything.

He will resonate
in the heart which melts and dissolves,
in the heart of faith which melts and dissolves.
He is the Almighty One who will resonate and resplend.
He is the One who knows your thoughts
before you think them.
He knows the minutes and the ages.
He knows birth and death.
He is within the Life within the life of all lives.
He is the Light known as the Truth.
He is the One who watches over and protects all life.
He is the Ocean of Compassion.
He is the Complete One known as Allāhu.
He is the One who belongs equally to all.
He is the One who belongs equally to all.
He is without ethnic group, religion, or separation.

He is the Pure One who is Almighty.
He exists as that One Power.
He is the Original One, unseen by any life.
He is the One who rules alone.

He is the Father to all the lives in the world.
Believe in Him.
Believe in Him.
Believe in Him.
Do not ever just pretend to believe in Him.
Do not ever pretend to believe in Him in the world.
Do not ever pretend to believe in Him.

Determinedly believe in Him.
Determinedly believe in Him.
Do not ever attempt to deceive Him or
pretend to believe in Him.
Do not ever pray pretending to believe in Him.
Do not pretend to pray.
Do not put on a pretense of
worshipping Him in the world,
a pretense of praying to Him in the world.
Do not ever pretend to believe in God.
Do believe in God,
Believe that He is the One who knows everything.
Have the absolute certitude that
He is intermingled in all lives.
Truly believe in Him.

He is the One who dwells in all lives.
He will help you
whether you are His friend or His enemy.
But Ādi, God, is the One who will
look at everything one day.
He is the One who will ask the questions

on the day that He calls you.
He is the One who knows right and wrong.
He is the One who understands and knows all lives.
He is the One who exists in the earth,
in the sky, and everywhere.
He is the One who is hidden in all the hidden lives.

He is the Fragrance in the flower.
He is the Taste in the fruit.
He is the Light in the eyes.
He is the Sweet Sound in the ears.
He is the One who realizes the fragrance in the nose.
He is the One who knows the taste on the tongue.
He is the One who exists as the Atom in the body.
He is the Father to all the worlds.

Believe in Him, believe in Him.
Do not ever pretend to believe in God.
Do not ever pretend to believe in Him.
Pretend to believe in the world.
Pretend to believe in the world,
but do not believe anything in the world,
do not believe anything in the world.
Believe in God, but do not ever pretend to believe in Him.
Believe in God, but do not ever pretend to believe in Him.
Do not ever pretend to believe in Him.

Do not believe in all the things you see. Do not believe in the
things you see and hear. Just pretend to believe in them. But do
not believe in them. Believe in God, but do not ever pretend to

believe in Him. The reason is that He is the One who knows everything. You should not try to deceive Him.

The blood, the body—do not believe in any of those things. Just say, "Okay, it's okay," and pretend to believe in them.

# Getting the Light Body

*Wednesday, January 18, 1979, 9:30 A.M.*

THERE IS NO USE for this body
other than for feasting, eating, sleeping,
other than for feasting, eating, sleeping,
other than for feasting, eating, sleeping,
howling about relatives and blood ties,
howling about the greatness of friends,
kinship, relatives, and blood ties.

It praises those who are learned,
and cries when the meaning of it all is obscure.
There is no use for this body.
There is no use for this body
other than for feasting, eating, and sleeping.
There is no use for it
other than for the shouting and howling about
belongings, possessions, relatives, and attachments,
belongings, possessions, relatives, and attachments,
titles, honors, positions, gold, wealth, land, buildings,
calves, cattle, buildings, and properties.
Except for its howling and howling and its disappearance,
there is no use for this body.
There is no use for this body.

O body that eats food and wanders about!
Flesh, blood, and fluid joined,
fluid and blood joined with flesh.
Fluid and blood,
air, fire, the colors, maya, mind, desire, and thought—
all these things have joined together
as one changing thing,
howling and yelling,
dividing itself into the "I" and the "you,"
saying, "mine" and "yours,"
howling and yelling,
praising and blaming.

It is through belongings, relatives,
attachments, and affections,
through blood ties,
through hunger, through illness,
through old age, and through death,
that this body is buried in selfishness.
There is no use for this body.
There is no benefit in this body for you.

It thinks and thinks and cries and cries,
wandering like a dog,
without knowing its purpose.
It simply eats like a cow and then disappears.
All the scenes you have seen,
all the scenes you have seen
are thoughts of dark maya, nothing else.

All the food you have eaten is hell.
Everything with which you have grown your body is a sin.
All the food you have eaten in order to grow your body
has eaten something else.
You became an embryo in sin and in darkness.
You have taken a form in the thoughts of
attachment, arrogance, karma, and maya,
in the form of the illusion of the animal qualities of
*tārahan, singhān,* and *sūran,*
the three sons of maya.
You took this birth, and
all these sections intermingled in the embryo.
That embryo grew
from blood, from fluids, from air, and from fire.

After that, after you were born,
it needed the same food in order to grow;
afterwards, you had to keep giving it
cattle, goats, asses, monkeys, horses, rats, cats,
hens, roosters, rats, cats, pigs —
you killed everything you saw for that embryo.
You sacrificed those bodies to your body,
and made meat the food for the meat of your body.

You gave meat as food to meat.
You gave water to water.
You gave air to air.
You gave fire to fire.
You gave blood to blood.
You gave earth to earth.

When you come to death, this stops,
and you begin to cry and shout, "What was it all for?"
All the houses, the forests, the gold,
the belongings you owned
will take their own forms and
become your hell
when you think of how you lived
and how there was no benefit
to be had from the actions of growing the body,
and how useful you believed it all to be.

You grew a deep hell inside of yourself,
and you grew in the depths of that hell.
You ate the food of that sacrificial pit.
You lay in that hell and died there.
In the state of the "I,"
you lived
divided by the "you" and the "I"
and demonstrated that.
You praised the "I."
You thought the whole country was your village and
gained enjoyment from it.
You thought that house belonged to you.
You called the animals that swallowed you, your relatives.

All of it has been useless.
Will you not realize that all of it has been useless?
There has been no benefit except for
the feasting, the eating, and the sleeping.

O man who grew the body!
Please realize this section and
endeavor to avoid all those sins.
Open your embryo and look into it.
Cut away the connection to your karma,
all those sinful thoughts, those sacrificial, evil actions.
Correct what you eat and feast upon.
Examine it and correct it.
Think and think of the way you were born,
look at what you ate and how you lived.

Realize that there is a form within you that is human.
There is another body within this body.
If you open it and look within,
you will see no evil, no kin,
no relatives, no attachment, no sin, no "I," no "you."
It will not kill or eat anything.
It will not live in sin.
It will not associate with maya.
It will not join with blood ties.
It will understand what the "I" and the "you" are
and push them aside.

That is the treasure of wisdom,
the body within wisdom,
the Light of the heart.
God will be within it,
and it will be a Light ray within God.
It will be a form in your house,
a Cage within the cage.
It will be a Light form.

That will be human,
that will be God,
that will be the completion of Light within your heart.
Realize that the form there is the form of Man.
Look at that form,
slip into it, and
do the duties of God, of Ādi.

Pray to God,
join with God,
join with God,
do God's duties,
do God's duties,
have His qualities,
have His actions, His conduct, His demeanor,
His goodness, and His love.
When you take them in and allow them to mature,
when you join with Him and dwell with Him,
it is on that day that your life will be a useful life.
That will be a useful life for you.

That life will join with the Treasure that will protect you.
That will be an eternal treasure house for you.
That will be the body of wisdom;
that will be the heaven in your heart.
You will be the owner of that house in the kingdom of God.
You will be the owner of God's house.
That will be the state of equality,
the state of giving peace to all lives,
the state of giving peace.
That will be the justice of the almighty perfection of God.

If you realize this state, then
this world, that world, and the world of pure souls—
all three worlds—will be the house of Light in which
you will dwell.
Then your body will dwell in
a state of Light in all three worlds.

Until you realize that the Light form is your form,
you will think this body is permanent.
You will think that this false body is permanent.
You will think the embryonic body is permanent.
You will think this karmic body is permanent.
You will think this arrogant body is permanent.
You will think this illusory body is permanent.

In order to grow this embryo of
earth, fire, water, and air that took form,
you will give it food and nourishment.
It will kill, feast, eat, and sleep.
There will be no other benefit.
Realize this.
Realize this, O man.
Realize and know this.
Know yourself; look at yourself.
Form the intention to be clear about this.

Join together on the path to God every day.
Search for your form.
Intend to do the duty of God.
That is our exaltedness, the house of our form.

My beloved ones, endeavor to realize this.
Destroy all your worldly obstinacy.
Remove the monkey that lives with you.
Endeavor to destroy those monkey tricks,
and you will see that the form of God is your form;
you will see the Light Form.
Inside yourself, you will see the body within the body
that is your body.
You will see your form as the body within the body.
You will see your body.

Try to stay within and dwell inside that body.
That will bring you eternal bliss and protect you.
*Āmīn.*
May it be so.

# Everything Will Happen As God Intends

*[Song to the mind and the mind's response]*

*Monday, July 21, 1980*

No MATTER WHAT we do,
no matter what we do,
no matter what we do,
it will all happen according to the divine grace of God.

No matter how we do it,
it will happen as God intends,
according to His actions.

There is love
and there is wealth within Him.
There is grace
and there is wealth within Him.
The love that protects us is within Him.
The love and the grace that protect us are within Him.

No matter what we do,
the grace of God, the love, the compassion, and
the blessing will be with us.
When He is our Protector, our Guardian,

when He is our Protector, our Guardian,
everything that happens to us will be His action.
Everything that happens to us will be His action.

O mind, know this.
O mind, know this.
Do not tremble.
Try to realize this.
Do not tremble.
Try to realize this.

If wisdom grows with faith in God and
with determination, if you have certitude,
if you place everything in
God's responsibility and then act,
if you place everything in
God's responsibility and then act,
He will understand everything,
and He will protect you.
He will watch over you.
He will take you to the shore.
He will take you on the good path towards Him.
Even if you go on the wrong path,
His protection will still be there.

Even if you follow
your mind, desire, and thoughts,
your mind, desire, and thoughts,
the visions of your eyes, and the visions of your mind,
He is the One who knows.

He is the One who knows the visions,
He is the One who knows the mind,
He is the One who knows the visions,
the One who understands the lives of all creations.
He is the One.

Therefore, He is the One who knows
the good and the evil that come to you,
the exaltedness and the degradation.
Because He knows everything,
it is His duty to protect you in any situation.

He is the One who does selfless duty.
He is the Chieftain who does not depend on
help from others.
He is the One who treats everything with equality.
He is the One who does what is good,
the Ruler of Grace,
the One who does what is good, the Ruler of Grace.

He is the God who does exist.
He is the God who does exist.
He is the One who understands your future state.
He is the One who knows what you will receive
before you receive it.
Therefore, the duty that He does will be for your good.

O mind, know this.
Realize this with clear wisdom, O mind.
Realize this with clear wisdom, O mind.

Do not tremble.
You, the mind that has been swallowed by
the visions of the eyes,
do not tremble.

When your desires, your attachments, your relationships,
your desires, your attachments, your relationships
are drawing you in and pulling on you,
when they torture you, torment you, and lead you astray,
He is the One who knows this state.
He is the One who knows you.
He is the One who knows your *qalb*, your heart,
your thoughts, your intentions, and the days of
your life that are yet to come,
who knows everything—your future and your past.
He is the One who has given you [the choice between]
exaltedness and degradation.
He can change and transform you, look.
O mind, He can change and transform you, look.

When He takes away one thing,
His intention is to give you another.
He will give you something better.
Through doing that, He will take away from you
a future evil.
He might take away your relationships, your attachments,
what you rely on, what you trust,
if they would cause suffering to you in the future.
He is the One who knows that.
Therefore, do not tremble, O mind.

You need patience, *sabūr, shukūr, tawakkul,*
inner patience, contentment, surrender to God.
Praise Him, with *al-hamd.*
Think of Him always.
Search for His responsibility.
Meet Him with love.
Later you will understand.
Later you will understand the great wealth
you have been given.

O mind, not everything you see is beautiful for you.
Not everything you see and hold on to is for your life.
Not everything you think of is a thought for you.
Not everything you focus on, look at,
or listen to is good for you.

Later you will realize, know, and be clear.
Analyze, realize, and see, O mind!
Analyze, realize, and see, O mind!
After that you will know the happiness of your life.

Believe! Everything that happens is His wealth.
Live! Place all your intentions in His responsibility.
Recite! It is He alone that you seek.
He will understand your thoughts and act for you, look.
He will understand your thoughts and act for you, look.
What He gives you will benefit you.
It will not perish for many millions of years,
look, O mind.

Do not be disturbed unnecessarily, O mind.
Do not feel pain because of your day-to-day thoughts.
Do not feel pain, O mind.

There is a Good Thing.
He is everywhere in the land,
everywhere, in everything, and in your cage.
If you think, you will understand.

Look at the Ruler of Grace who rules the three worlds.
Place your focus upon Him.
Establish your love within His love.
Send your wisdom into His wisdom.
Lock your conduct into His conduct.
Place your qualities into His qualities.
He will be your Guru and
guide you on the path with grace, look, O mind.

After that, He will give you the good path.
He will support you and
hold you in His hands day and night.
He will always bring you success.
Then you can attain success for your life in
this world and the next.
You can attain success for your life in
this world and the next, O mind.

All the evils of which we are unaware
come in the form of desire to attack us.
Ignorance, maya, and mind join together
and sneak into our hearts.

Mind and desire will take us to the deepest jungle.
Blood ties and attachments,
attachments to relatives and woman and wealth,
physical visions and all the thoughts
attached themselves to me
when I was in embryonic form.
They caught me.
Now they are tormenting and torturing me.

I am like a man electrocuted.
The current of maya has come into and spread throughout
my nerves, my skin, my flesh.

This is the current that runs in the blood.
The current of maya is torturing me.
These currents have captured me, held me, and
squeezed out my life.

They have changed my true states.
They have changed my relationship with
the God who has created me.
They have changed my love,
the grace and the qualities of my Father.
They have changed the truth,
they have changed the wisdom.

They have imprisoned me inside thoughts of
hypnotic delusion and maya.
This current has buried me and
is burning me with hot coals

throughout my body, my nerves, my flesh,
skin, bones, and marrow,
spreading everywhere, running, running, capturing me,
tormenting me.
This suffering is turning the earthly cage of my body black.

It is subjecting me to suffering,
tormenting me through these attachments,
through these blood ties,
through desire for earth, woman, and gold, and
through attachments to kin.
All these forms of the darkness of ignorance
have become the countless demons
that have crept into my heart.

They make me run here and there,
They do not leave me for half a second.
I am in a state without peace or tranquility.
I am in a state without peace or tranquility,
a state of not thinking about the One who
has existed then and now.

Even if I think of Him,
my desire, my attachments, and my blood will
intermingle with that thought;
that thought will not stand with certitude.
They will still be able to torture and torment me.

Like a tornado uprooting a tree,
like a tornado uprooting a tree,

the demons and ghosts in my mind are torturing me.
Religions, races, blood ties, attachments, relationships,
intentions, desires, lust, hatred, the arts, the sexual games,
colors and hues and beauty,
all of them enter into me as desires,
torturing and tormenting me.
They do not let me think of You for even a second,
for even a second.

The maya, this current of maya is whirling,
surrounding me, spinning me, breaking me,
squeezing me, sucking me dry.
This illusory world comes as a current
that contains all the connections to hell.
This state is causing me unbearable pain.
I am convulsing like a worm
that has received an electric shock,
convulsing day and night.

O God, I am forgetting You.
I am screaming, *"Aiyō! Aiyō! Aiyō! Ah! Hah! Ah!"*
howling and wailing.
I cry and cry day and night.
I shout about my wealth, happiness, titles, positions,
the wife, the children, the calf and the cow,
the house, the children, the calf and the cow.
Thinking of the earth and the sky and
these attachments that bind me to them,
I suffer.

This is ruining me,
melting down my heart, making it tremble.
It is turning me into waves on a fathomless ocean.
It is burying me in the darkness of ignorance.
It is burying me in the darkness of ignorance.

I am blind.
I am deaf.
I am mute—
this mouth that should speak truth has become mute.
Wisdom, this tongue, and this *qalb* that should speak justly
have been hidden.
Fascinated by the darkness of ignorance, they now tell lies.
They make me lie and bear false witness.
They make me bear false witness.
The truth is hidden.
The religions of the world bear false witness.
Book knowledge makes me
accept unacceptable things, bearing false witness,
saying, "There is no truth."
The heart is a witness.
Mesmerized,
I commit all the evil actions possible in my life.
Having forgotten God's Truth,
I become a victim to indescribable suffering.
It is making me tremble.

O Father, cut off this state.
Take me beyond it so that I may reach the feet of God.
Dispel this magnetic current from my *qalb*.

Destroy the illusion.
Destroy the evils that come from the connection
to illusion and all the karma.
Give me the path to attain peace,
the state of equality, a tranquil life.
Destroy my thoughts that are like bubbles in water.
Correct this mind that loves all the impermanent things.
Give us conscience, exaltedness, and wisdom.
Make my qualities beautiful and make me act accordingly.
Give me Your three thousand gracious qualities,
a life without attachments,
selfless duty,
actions and conduct without malice or envy, and
selfless actions.
Cut away the evil,
so that I may do my duties according to
Your ninety-nine *wilāyāt* that are Your duty,
so that I can do them with gracious qualities.

Give me Your grace, give me the kingdom of grace.
At this moment when
maya has broken me,
and everything has tumbled down around me —
this very second,
come to protect me.

Look at me, take me to the shore,
O Able One, O Ruler of Grace, O Incomparable Love.
O God, You are the One who bestows
the undiminishing wealth of grace.

Come!
Allāhu! Make my resonating *qalb* resonate and resonate.
Give me the wisdom to understand.
Give me the Nūr, the Light, the completion of wisdom.
Give me Your grace so that my *qalb* can attain
the perfection of completion.
O Padishāh, O King of Kings, O God, Allāhu!

Give me Your grace so that I may live as a human being,
so that I may live as a human being,
so that I may have human qualities in this world,
doing duty and giving peace to all the lives in this world.
Help me to attain justice and peace,
so that I recognize all lives as my own life
and do duty in a state of peace.
Give me Your grace
so that I attain a state of duty and service.

Will You do this with Your grace?
You are the One without any parallel or equal, Allāhu.
You are the wealth that never diminishes.
Unchanging Truth, Bliss of Grace!
Unfailing Justice!
During a life of all eternity,
You are the One who has never deviated from integrity.

Dwell in my *qalb* as the Truth within truth,
so that I may do Your duty without limit,
so that I can enter into all lives,
knowing their thoughts and intentions,

knowing their thoughts and intentions,
knowing the focus of their *qalbs,*
understanding the visions seen by their eyes,
understanding their goals.
O dutiful God!
Give me Your duty, Your goal,
and Your thoughts with Your grace.
Give me the protection of wisdom to have
compassion for all lives.
Protect me and give me the grace.
O Perfection, O Absolute Completion, Allāhu.
*Āmīn.*
May it be so.

# This World Is a Prayer Mat

*Monday, August 4, 1980, 9:23 A.M.*

*[Recording begins here.]*

HE IS A RESOURCEFUL PERSON. One who can perform his own act well is a resourceful person.

> O Man, the world is a stage for drama.
> Realize this.
> O Man, the world is a stage for drama.
> Realize this.
> Realize this.
> There are many actors.
> Know this and see this.
>
> There are four hundred trillion,
> four hundred trillion, ten thousand types of actors,
> dancers, singers, and writers —
> singers, dancers, writers,
> those who have scientific wisdom,
> those who have false wisdom,
> those who lack wisdom,
> those who have scientific wisdom,
> and those who have true wisdom.

There are those who practice sexual arts.
They are all performing artists.
There are those who practice sexual arts.
They are all performing artists.
Those who find happiness in the world,
those who act out the desires of their minds,
they all exist. They all exist.

Some of them will dance,
some of them will sing,
some of them will play games,
and run, run towards the sexual games.
They will perform the arts.
They will speak of artistic wisdom.
They will play in the realms of
*indira jālam, mantira jālam,* and maya *jālam.*[1]

They will walk on water.
They will fly in the sky.
They will walk on water.
They will fly in the sky.
They will wander about invisible to the eyes of others.
They will wander about invisible to the eyes of others.
They will capture demons,
they will talk with dogs.
They will capture demons,
they will talk with dogs.

---

1. *indira jālam* (phrase) the magic of maya which extends into space; *mantira jālam* (phrase) magic performed through the use of mantras; maya *jālam* (phrase) the magical performances of illusion

They will ride horses.
They will join with monkeys.
They will join with monkeys.
They will dance, they will praise each other.
They will laugh, they will cry.
They will twist the earth into a rope.
They will bend the sky into a bow.
They will twist the earth into a rope.
They will bend the sky into a bow.
They will act to obtain the praise of the world.
They will take the body to hell.
They will reveal the body and praise it.
They will take the body to hell.
They will think unthinkable thoughts and kill.
They will strike and kill anyone.

They will turn in any direction and guide others to it.
They will hurt anyone.
They will kill animals and eat them.
They will torture other lives and call it praiseworthy.
They will accumulate money and wealth.
They will make the earth-world their own.
They will present themselves as great people.
They will present their acts as
the best acts in the entire world.
They will wander about everywhere and guide others.
They will consider themselves the best actors in the world.
They will do this with seeming wisdom and intelligence.
They will be praised and criticized.
They will be seen everywhere.

O humankind, realize this and look at it.
They will forget themselves and play,
as they fly and wander about everywhere in this world.
No matter how many things they do:
they may fly in the sky,
they may even perform the miracles of
a *munivar* or a *gnāni*,[2]
they may even perform the miracles of
a *munivar* or a *gnāni*,
no matter what they do,
they will never know the exaltedness of
controlling the mind and just being still.
They will never know the exaltedness of
controlling the mind and just being still.

Such a person will creep into the place of birth.
He will creep back into the place of birth.
He will demonstrate how to be a father.
He will say, "I am the father" and demonstrate that.
He will go to that place and forget that it was his mother.
He will later call it wife.
With sexual frenzy he will hold the breast
from which he suckled and drank milk.
He will seize it with lust.
He will seize everything he looks at in that sexual frenzy.
Mesmerized, he will run in the game of lust played by
mind and desire,
fall into the sperm, and merge with karma.

---

2. *munivar* (n.) an ascetic; *gnāni* (n.) a wise man

Afterwards he will creep into hell.
He will search for a house.
After that he will search for a cow and a calf,
a wife, a child, and a house, a cow and a calf,
a wife, a child, and a house.
He will search for wealth, health, money, and cash.
He will promise to conduct himself well.

Look at these actors in the world.
Look at how they play their parts in the world:
the miracles these actors perform as they play their parts.
These are the miraculous acts of the actors.
Hey, these are the miraculous acts!
But it is rare and exalted for someone to
control his mind and just be still.
It is rare and exalted for someone to
control his mind and just be still.

They have forgotten the God
who rules the heart and
who exists as wisdom within wisdom,
wisdom within wisdom.
They have forgotten that God.

They will dance on this stage and establish their fame.
They will dance on this stage and establish their fame.
They will praise themselves, saying "I, I."
They will praise themselves, saying "I, I,"
raising the flag of fame.
Men in this state will live in this world.

Men in this state will live in this world,
establish their fame, and
be buried in the earth.
In the end, they will be buried in the earth and
merged with it.
They will become fodder for fire, earth, water, air.
In the end, they will burn in the fire of hell.
They will burn.
O man, do not believe in this stage.
Do not think that this act has any power.
Do not think that this act has any power.

There is One who is inside.
Look inside, there is an Atom.
Look within it for the Mystery.
Look inside, there is an Atom.
Look within it for the Mystery
within yourself.
If you realize it and understand it with wisdom,
there will be a Mystery.
Place yourself inside it,
burn through it with wisdom and then look at it.

After earth and sky die,
after earth, woman, and gold die within you,
after the "I" within the self has been buried,
you will see with your wisdom that it is
only He who exists.
That is the day on which you will become His slave.
That is the one Mystery you must see in your cage.

It is a Secret your eyes, nose, and mouth do not see.
It is the one Secret of your birth.
The meaning of that understanding is a Mystery.
If you can understand that Mystery,
it will be your life, eternal life, eternal life.
It will always be alive.

Living without birth or death,
you will be a good person, a good person
in all the universes,
a good person, a good person,
a good person, a good person
to all lives.
You will be a good person.
You will be the one who serves all lives.
You will be the one who dwells
commingled in all lives, serving them,
giving them peace, showing them tranquility.
You will reach peace within yourself,
and you will show peace and tranquility to all lives.

You will perform your duties
in the earth-world, in the sky-world, and
in the world of pure souls.
You will live as the loving one doing duty in
the world of pure souls.
O Man, you will live as the beloved to all lives.
Then you will become a messenger of
that One who is an Atom.
Then you will become a messenger of

that One who is an Atom.
Realize the mysterious Secret,
realize this Mystery, Him,
this Secret, and yourself, O Man.
Realize this.

Until you understand this meaning,
everything will be an act in this world for you,
an act with many dramas.

They will all be actors on this stage of God.
They will all be actors on this stage of the act of
creation in the world.
They will all be actors.
They will all be actors.
Each one will dance, look for praise,
enjoy it, and laugh, O humankind.
Each one will dance, look for praise, gain fame, and
establish fame on this stage.

O humankind! God will watch.
There will come a day! God is watching your act.
He is the One watching your act.
Everyone is an actor,
but no one *here* watches your act.
Because everyone in this world is an actor,
everyone an actor seeking the prize,
everyone an actor seeking the prize,
acting and asking for titles and fame.

Everyone is an actor.
No one here watches the act.
There is no one watching you act.
Each person acts, praises himself,
dances, enjoys it, and laughs.
Each person acts, praises himself,
dances, enjoys it, laughs,
and sees the greatness in himself,
O humankind.

Soon there will come a day,
there will come a day when the act is over,
there will come a day when the act is over.
After the acts and the costumes are removed,
in which house will you dwell?
O Man, realize which one.

On the day you take your innate form—
whether you acted in dog form,
a cat, a rat, a monkey, a demon, or a ghost form,
an elephant, a monkey, an ass, or a swine,
a wolf, a fish, or a rat—
whatever act you performed,
after the act is over,
you will see the body that is known as your hell.

After you remove the costume,
you will see your birth,
arrogance, karma, and maya in the end.

You will see the illusory form of
*tārahan, singhan,* and *sūran,*
the three sons of maya.
Lust, hatred, miserliness, greed, fanaticism, and envy,
you will see these six evils.

You will see the five sins —
intoxicants, sexual passion, theft, murder, and falsehood —
as your connection to karma.
These seventeen evils will join together and
become the seventeen worlds in which you danced.
These are the *purānas,*[3] the acts, and the sexual games.
These are the *purānas,* the sixty-four sexual games,
the sixty-four arts, the sixty-four arts of dance,
the songs you sang, and the games in which you ran.

When your dance is done and you look around,
you will see only karma, maya, and arrogance.
O man, realize and see.
Know the dance and the act you are performing.
Know the dance and the act you are performing,
and then try to dance.

For a person of wisdom, this is a prayer mat.
For a person without wisdom,
it is a stage for the performance of
four hundred trillion miracles.

---

3. *purānas* (n.) The seventeen evil qualities within man. [Lit. an ancient story, a legendary tale or myth]

For a person without wisdom,
it is a stage for the performance of
four hundred trillion, ten thousand miracles.
O man, for a person of wisdom,
this world is a prayer mat.
Understand and see this, O man.
Understand and see this, O man.

On the day that you understand and act
on this prayer mat,
if you understand, know this, and act on this prayer mat,
the One who created you, the One who gives you food,
the One who gives you life, the One who protects you,
the One who calls you back in the end
will look at your act, overflow with happiness, and smile.
He will be happy and smile.
He will be happy and embrace you to His heart.
He will embrace you heart to heart and call to you,
"O My son, precious jeweled light of My eyes!
My Light!
Master of My kingdom!
Chieftain of truth!
You are the chieftain of all lives in the world, who
gives justice to My creations!"

He will give you the body of His kingdom.
He will judge you and give you that
kingdom of *daulah,* of wealth.
He will look at your acts with happiness,
your acts of prayer.

He will realize your splendor, and
give you the crown,
give you the crown of *gnānam,* of divine knowledge.
He will give you the splendor.
He will give you exaltedness in your life.
He will give you eternal life without birth or death.
Now and forever in all worlds,
you can live having reached peace,
having attained the power of
the completion of absolute Light.

O Man, look at that state.
Realize the story into which you came, finish it,
and know the secret of life.
Understand your Father's mystery.
When you understand yourself and lose yourself,
understanding the Master who is your Father,
worship Him, pray to Him, pray to Him,
bow before Him, and join with Him,
that will be the most exalted point in your life.

This world is a prayer mat,
a prayer mat that has been given to you.
O Man of wisdom, please understand this.
Then you will understand the secret of your birth.
Then you will reach the Mystery that is your Father.
On that day you will attain liberation and bliss.
*Āmīn. Āmīn.*
May it be so. May it be so.

# Grant Us This Blessing

*Thursday, March 5, 1981, 6:45 A.M.*

ALLĀHU, Allāhu, Allāhu!
So that Your resonance resonates,
so they see You and bow down before You
with melting *qalbs*, with melting hearts,
may all the *qalbs* of my children, all their *qalbs*,
melt like wax.

So that they set their intention upon You and
pray to You with melting *qalbs*,
You must stay in their *qalbs*,
make their *qalbs* melt,
protect them, nurture them, and watch over them.

O Jeweled Light of Our Eyes,
come, destroy the karma of our birth.
Dispel all the evils that have caught hold of us,
that are shaking us.
Give us Your grace, give us Your milk,
give us Your love, give us Your love,
embrace us and comfort us,
grant us this blessing.
Allāhu!

Cut away our connection to
the thoughts belonging to maya and
the blood ties that flow throughout the mind.
Cut away all desire for earth,
desire for woman,
desire for gold,
desire for possessions.
Dispel them from our hearts,
dispel them from us.
Fill us instead with the Light of grace,
with divine luminous Light
and the Light of Your love.
Grant us this blessing.

O Father of divine luminous bliss!
My God without birth or death, Allāhu!
O Thought within thought,
the Certainty and the Clarity in the dream,
the One who bestows the perception,
O our Creator,
O Divine Grace,
Allāhu!

You are the One who knows the heart,
who knows the action,
who knows the conduct,
who knows all my thoughts.
Come, instruct us as the Gnāna Guru[1] who

---

1. Gnāna Guru (phrase) the Teacher of divine wisdom

dwells in and understands
the knowledge of all the heavenly realms.
Ruler of All Things,
Wealth of Wisdom,
Almighty One who rules the three worlds,
illAllāhu!

May our bodies melt,
may our *qalbs* melt.
May they melt within us,
may wisdom and love melt together and intermingle.
May our faith and determination melt into Your grace,
may all of our intentions settle into You,
may we dwell in Your beauty.

May we commingle with Your Light and dwell there,
embracing all who embrace You.
Grant us the grace to intermingle with love.
Make this complete within us
and everlasting.
Make it peaceful and tranquil,
make it the *sabūr* of peace,
intermingling as patience,
*shukūr*, gratitude, and *tawakkul*, surrendering
into that which You gave to us in trust.

Establish in our *qalbs* the word *al-hamd*[2]
that will praise you.

2. *al-hamd* (Arabic n.) the praise; the five letters, *alif, lām, mīm, hā', and dāl,* of the
   Arabic alphabet, which form the heart

Give us the right to dwell with You.
Grant us this blessing!
Cut away birth.
Cut away death.
Cut away the ninety-six obsessions
that arise from the bile.
Cut away the mind.
Cut away the actions of the mind.
Cut away all the divisive thoughts—
you are different / I am different.
Cut away the qualities that exist separately, separately.
Cut away that thing we call fate.
Cut away that thing we call fate.
Give us living wisdom.
Comfort us and grant us Your grace,
Allāhu!

May we intermingle with You,
one with the One.
May we merge with You,
hold firm to the one path,
worship You,
bow down before You,
and intermingle with You.
Grant us this birthright.
Grant us this blessing,
Allāhu!

Stay in all my children,
resonate in the hearts of my children.

Resonate!
Resplend!
Dwell,
and establish Yourself
in their hearts!
Dwell,
and establish Yourself within them!

Intermingle with them inside and outside,
in their eyes,
in the pupils of their eyes,
in the light within their eyes,
in their ears,
in their noses,
in their mouths,
in the taste on their tongues,
in their wisdom,
in their love,
in their determination,
in their certitude,
in their thoughts, and
in their lives.

Merge inside their lives as Light.
Make them into forms of Light.
Stay inside them and show them the way.
Grant them this blessing.
Open the way.
Show them how to discern the right from the left.

Make them understand good and evil.
Show them the *dunyā* and the *ākhirah,*
this world and God's kingdom.
Make them live as free human beings.
O most pure One,
yā Allāhu!

Make them go beyond the mind,
beyond the woman of the mind,
beyond the state of the desire of the mind,
beyond the mesmerism,
beyond the fluid shadow of the mind,
beyond the thoughts of the mind,
beyond the tricks of the monkey mind.

O Primal One who exists beyond, beyond the three worlds,
who has transcended the three times,
show them the state
that intermingles and dwells with You.
Show them the state.
Show them the grace.
Show them peace and tranquility in their lives.
While they are still alive,
grant them their birthright of
calmness, tranquility, peace, and
exalted lives.

Make them understand within themselves
the right and the left breath so they can
sit in meditation,

mingle with You, and
converse with You.
Give them the right to intermingle within You
and to dwell within You.
Grant them this blessing,
O God, Complete Perfection,
the One who rules internally and externally,
Allāhu!

You are the One who dwells in
everything,
everywhere,
here,
there,
in me,
in you.

Stay within my children
as the Light of Grace,
as the Divine Luminous Light,
as the Light of love,
as the Divine Light,
as the Divine Gem,
as the Gem that is the Guru,
as the Bliss of Grace that fills their hearts.

O Lord of Divine Luminous Bliss,
Resplendent Pearl of Light,
Gem of the three worlds that
has transcended all supernatural powers,

come,
intermingle in the hearts of my children,
in their bodies
in their lives,
internally and externally,
in their eyes, and
in the pupils of their eyes.
Have compassion for them.

Cut away all the karmic evils of the world.
Be the One who sits with closed eyes
in silence within them,
stopping the many visions in their *qalbs.*
O great and exalted formless One
who knows the meaning,
Almighty One,
illAllāhu.

Loving God,
Brilliance of Grace,
Allāhu!
Lord of indivisible and perfect completion,
O God,
Allāhu!

Do not forsake us.
Grant us Your grace.
Protect us.
Grant us this blessing,
grant us this blessing.

Grant liberation to our souls.
You Yourself must grant this.
Show us the way
with peace and tranquility.
Make us know that life is like a bubble in the water,
this life that is being destroyed
by blood ties and attachments.

May we leave it behind.
May You take us beyond this.
Give us
an imperishable life,
a life of wisdom,
a life of clarity,
a life of Light, and
the completion that is everlasting.
Give us the completion.
May You, Yourself,
grant us the blessing of peace in life,
in our lives.

God of Grace,
Light of Grace residing within love!
State of Bliss,
come,
grant us refuge,
grant us grace,
protect us,
grant us this blessing.

O my Eye,
Gem of Light,
Almighty One who knows the pupil of the eye,
end the suffering of the poor.
Cut away all our evils.
Gather us at Your feet.
Make our lives grow,
while we are still alive.
You are the One who existed then and who exists now,
intermingled in Truth,
existing as the One.
May wisdom, the soul, and You intermingle,
One with the other.

May we live with determination.
May You make our hearts clear.
Almighty One, Ruler and Protector of the three worlds.
illAllāhu!
Yā Rabbal-'ālamīn!
O Ruler of the universes.
Yā Rahmān!
O Compassionate One.
Yā Rabbal-'ālamīn!
Yā Rahmān!
Yā Rahmān!

You are the letter of wisdom
amongst the five letters.
Amongst the letters of the heart
You are the everlasting letter

known as Allāhu.
Protect us.
O Resplendent Completion,
You exist as the Completion within completion.

Give us peace and tranquility.
Dispel our evils.
Cut away our birth,
cut away our death,
cut away all the obsessions that arise from the bile.
Cut away all the support and the evil of the world.
O Pure One!
Give us Your beauty, Your help, Your grace;
give us only Your support.

Stand as our certitude in the search
to find clarity with You.
My heart is melting from the duties I am performing.
I am doing the duty of grace.
I am intermingled with You,
doing service to the Guru, to You.
I am doing service to the world.
I am doing Your beautiful service
and living as a righteous person.
Grant me the Light of certitude.

Change the goals and the evils of the body.
Open the truth,
and reveal it to us.
May goodness always be my life.

May I worship You day and night,
pray to You
so that I can
merge with You and speak with You.
O Jeweled Light of my Eye,
You Yourself must grant me this favor in fullness.
Show us the completion
of the state in which to worship You,
in which to pray to You.
Grant us this blessing.
Grant us this blessing,
O my Allāhu!
Allāhu!
Yā Rabbal-'ālamīn.
O God!
*Āmīn.*
Yā Rabbal-'ālamīn.
We need Your help always
in our lives and in our bodies.

Intermingle in the hearts of my children.
Protect them,
so they can do the duties of the straight path.
Give them the certitude and the faith and the completion.
Protect them.
Grant them this blessing.
O God of our intention,
Allāhu!

Give us Your compassion.
Help us always.
Forgive the faults my children have committed:
the faults they committed in the past
and the faults they will commit in the future,
the mistakes they made in the past
and the mistakes they will make in the future.
Pardon them.
Show them and establish for them
the path with peace and tranquility.
Grant them the grace
to stand and pray to You, to worship You—
make them exalted in this way.
Give them Your grace,
protect them,
grant them this blessing,
Allāhu.

*Āmīn.*
Yā Rabbal-'ālamīn.
May it be so.
O Creator of All the Universes.

# If We Become His Slaves
# We Can Overcome Even Death

*Tuesday, May 1, 1984, 9:00 A.M.*

THE ATTACHMENTS and blood ties,
the attachments and blood ties of
mind and desire, mind and desire,
mind and desire, mind and desire
do not know,
nor does the mind know that
there is a God who does exist,
there is a God who does exist.

Is there no human being who knows this?
O Man, do you not know this?
There is a God that
mind, desire, and thought do not know.
Do you not know this, O Man, do you not know this?
There is a God in an unknown place,
a place unknown to you.
O Man, there is a God in an unknown place.
Do you not know this, O Man?

The name of the One we call God is
beyond all boundaries.

One of His names is
the Lord of Liberation Beyond All Difficulties.
It is after all the evils are dispelled and
destiny is defeated that
His name is God.

He dwells intermingled in the heart,
in clarity, and in everything.
He speaks words of sweet nectar,
He gives milk to everything,
He treats everyone with equality.

The One who acts with this goodness
has a name and that name is God.
The One who acts with this goodness
has a name and that name is God.

He belongs in common to all lives, yet is
Unique among all things.
He belongs in common to all lives, yet is
Unique among all things.

Inside and outside, inside and outside,
He is Light.
As the Life within life,
He is the Friend within the body.
As the Life within life,
He is the beautiful Light within the body,
the Beauty that has obtained the soul's freedom,
the Beauty that has obtained the soul's freedom.

As the Mother, as the Father,
He is the God who dwells within us
without the six evils,
without anyone else.
He is the God who dwells within us
without the six evils,
without anyone else.
Do you not know this, O man?
Do you not know this, O man?

In this world, in this world,
can you take water from a pond with your bottle,
can you take water from a pond with your bottle,
without moving the water,
without moving the water?

It will move in your bottle and in the pond.
It will move in your bottle and in the pond.
Water will move,
will it not, will it not, will it not?

God dwells as the Life within all lives.
If you fall into Him,
your sorrows will be His sorrows.
To God,
all the sorrows of the world
are like water that fills a pond.
To God,
all the sorrows of all the creations of the world
are like water that fills a pond.

God takes
all the sorrows of all the creations of the world
that are like water that fills a pond.
He discards everything that must be discarded and
lives as the clear and mighty Ocean of Compassion.
He clears up all the dirt and
lives as the clarity of the might of the Ocean of Compassion.

He is the Origin of Compassionate Justice.
He is the Origin of Compassionate Justice.
He is the Master of the Three Thousand Blessings.
He is the Master of the Three Thousand Blessings.

He is the Original One
who dispels fate and assessment[1] and
who bestows the grace.
He is the Original One
who dispels fate and assessment and
who bestows the grace.

Do you not know the state in which
He shares what is within you?
Do you not know that He takes a share of your sorrow?
Do you not know that He takes a share of your sorrow?
Put all the illnesses and diseases

---

1. Fate and assessment: in Tamil, *vidiyum madiyum. Vidi* is fate or destiny. *Madi* is the fourth level of wisdom, the function of which is to begin to ask questions, to assess what it is that is being experienced and why we came to this world. It estimates what is going on in our lives and how much time we have here to do what we came to do. It makes choices based on these estimates, and these choices become fate.

that originate from everything you have collected
into Him,
put them into Him, and
then the effect of what you have taken into your bottle,
into your *qalb,*
then the effect of what you have gathered
will diminish;
your illnesses will diminish.

Your *qalb* will move,
just as water moves in a bottle.
You have taken in the movement of the pond:
have you not seen it move, become still and clear?
That is why One in that state is God.

All lives fall into Him;
they fall into the water,
they drink, they bathe, and they go.
No matter how many waves they create,
the movement will cease;
it will become still and clear.
One who has attained that state is God.

Your *qalb* exists in a state
like that of a small bottle,
in which the writing on the water is in constant motion.

If you fall into Allāh's responsibility
in prayer, in *toluhay,* in *'ibādah,*[2]

---

2. *toluhay,* (n.) prayer, worship; most often refers to the formal five-times prayer in Islām; *'ibādah* (Arabic n.) worship and service to God

with your intentions and with your focus,
with your thoughts and with your ideas,
if you take in His intention,
if you fall into Him and scoop up what is within Him,
what will come to you will depend upon
the capacity of your heart;
it will be similar to filling a bottle with water, with water.

If you fall into Him and pray,
it will all depend upon the capacity of your heart—
what you take from Him
will depend upon your capacity.

At first your heart will move as water moves;
then it will become still.
When the movement of the heart becomes still,
you too will become clear.
Then you too will become clear,
and the path to peace will appear before you.

Then prayer and the state of determination
will be firmly established within you.
Then God's name will resonate within you.
The grace of the Protector of Both Worlds
will begin to flow.

Do not blather, O Man,
in a state lacking understanding and knowledge.
Do not blather, O Man,
in a state lacking understanding and knowledge.

O Man created as *pahut arivu,* as divine analytic wisdom,
do not blather without understanding, O Man.

There is a God in a place
that mind, desire, and thought do not know;
do you not know this, O Man?
There is a God in a place
that you do not know;
do you not know this, O Man?

The name Allāhu is given to
the Treasure that never diminishes
no matter how much is taken from it.
The name Allāhu is given to
the Treasure that never diminishes
no matter how much is taken from it.

That Grace is available to everyone.
That Grace is available to everyone.
It is a Treasure that fills the heart.
That Grace is available to everyone.
It is a Treasure that is available to everyone.

Anyone who wishes, anyone who wants
can take this Grace.
Anyone who wishes, anyone who wants
can take this Grace.

The *qalbs* of those who do not want it are empty houses.
The *qalbs* of those who do not want it are empty houses.

If you establish yourself on the path of justice,
that beauty will come to you.

If you lose the path of justice,
darkness will come to your life.
It will become a karmic house of
lust, hatred, miserliness, and greed.
If you grasp those reins and act with those qualities,
you will be ruined in the end.
If you grasp those reins and act with those qualities,
you will be ruined in the end.

Allāhu is a Treasure
that belongs equally to everyone:
*Allu!* Take!
It is a Treasure that never diminishes
no matter how much is taken from it.
It is eternally beautiful, look!
It is eternally beautiful, look!

That Treasure will bring you freedom.
It is completion for one who seeks freedom.
For the *qalb* of one who seeks freedom, it is completion.
For those who have *īmān*, it is Light.
For those who know the heart, it is food.

For those who have transcended
mind, desire, and thought,
it is a crown, a crown of *gnānam*.
It is the Treasure of that King, that King,

that King who is the Rahmān.
It is the Treasure of that King who is the Rahmān.

We can attain that Grace whenever we want.
It is the Treasure that belongs in common to everyone.
It is the powerful Treasure that has
no race, religion, or prejudice.
It is the powerful Treasure of Bliss that has
no race, religion, or prejudice.

It is the food for all lives.
He grants that Grace before an eye can open and close.
If He were not giving it,
everything everywhere would be dead.
If He were not giving it,
everything everywhere would be dead.

Everyone, think and reflect.
See how the one Treasure that is God does exist.
Everyone, try to think!
Think of the one Treasure that is God, and listen.

Say it without saying it in your heart.
Sing to that One who is free, yā Rabbal-'ālamīn.
Sing to that One who is free, yā Rabbal-'ālamīn.
The bliss will come to you day and night.
You can obtain the help of the Ruler of Grace.
Look here.

He will always be the only One for us.
He is the One who exists as God, our Friend,
our Beloved, our Life, look.
He will come as our Shaikh and as our Sayyid, listen.
The One who dwells in all three worlds
will come as Grace,
the One who dwells in all three worlds
will come as Grace.
He is the One with the Open Heart, look.

The One who lives in the *qalb* is our Creator, listen.
He is the Compassionate Almighty One,
yā Rabbal-'ālamīn.
The One who lives in the *qalb* is our Creator, listen.
He is the One who is Compassionate Justice, look.

He is the One who lives there as Love within love.
He is the One who dwells intermingled with all lives.
He is the One who acts with
words and deeds that are the same.
He is the God who transcends
the imaginable and the unimaginable.

He will dwell within those who know Him.
He will be a great distance away from
those who do not know him, look.
He will be far away, look.

He will live with us there.
Whenever we think of Him, He will come closer.

When we realize this, He will gently enter into us.
If we believe in the truth, He will speak with us.

As we speak and speak with Him,
peace will come to us.
The more we are with Him,
the more our needs will decrease.
The more we embrace and embrace Him,
the more our sorrows will leave us.

If we become His *'abds,* His slaves,
we can overcome even death, look.
If we become His slaves and serve Him,
we can overcome even death, look.
*Āmīn. Āmīn. Āmīn.*
Yā Rabbal-'ālamīn.
May it be so. May it be so. May it be so.
O Creator of All the Universes.

# Why Didn't You Think of This Before?

*Monday, November 10, 1985, 8:23 P.M.*

THIS PERSON IS not here,
that person is not here.
These belongings are not here,
those belongings are not here.

Everyone who has come here,
the young and the old,
the babies just born,
the oldest men and those in their prime
will fall like flowers from a tree,
disappearing like fruit and leaves from a tree.

*Maname,* O my mind-self,
all the beings that have been born will die, curl up,
and leave this earth-world.
No matter how many possessions and belongings,
attachments and blood ties,
relationships and friendships they possess,
when they go, they will not tell anyone.
They will not tell us where they are going.
They will not tell us where they will be.

No one knows where, where they will go.
Where, where have they gone?
No one knows.

They will not speak or breathe.
They will not say anything after they leave.
Even if we cry and cry as we ask them, and
even if rivers of tears flow from their eyes,
only the tears will flow,
but they will not say anything at all.
Those who came here have gone,
those who are still here will disappear in the same way.
All those we saw are no longer visible now.

Those who once saw them now dance and sing,
"Those belongings are gone.
These belongings are gone.
Their livestock, cattle, and houses are gone."
As soon as they depart,
 everyone comes spinning, whirling, and running, saying,
"Mine! Mine! These are my belongings now."

They strike each other,
 grasping, pushing, shoving, and plundering.
They break each other's heads.
They break each other's heads.
They break each other's arms and legs.
They take their plunder and run.
Yet, in the end, nothing is left.

We do not see those who plundered and left.
We do not see those who searched for and
then hid their belongings.
We do not see those who looked on.
We do not see the rows and rows of those who
then hid their belongings.

For one who has lived in the world like this,
there is nothing.
He has no help, none.
Wherever he goes, he will be lost.
He has forgotten his Father,
and lies mesmerized in the seven seas of the world.
He lies mesmerized in the seven seas of the world,
jumping, twitching, dancing, wandering.
He has no one.

Those who come will come.
Those who came before us will go.
Those who come will go.
Those who come will depart.
Those who are here are still alive.
This is the state of the world, Father—
decorated.
This is the state in which the world lives, Father—
decorated.

Yet it is not the world that speaks.
It is man who makes the world speak and move.
He decorates it and makes it beautiful.

He adorns himself for the dance.
He decorates himself and stands there as an actor;
he sings and dances.
Those who are still here
are hypnotized by
the sixty-four sexual games,
the sixty-four arts and sciences,
the acting and the dancing.
They are fascinated by their own acts,
mesmerized by the dancing and singing.
They dance in the world.

The world is a stage.
He is the actor upon it,
the actor who performs the dance.
Man is the actor.
The world is his stage,
decorated by the sixty-four sexual games.
His jewels are the sixty-four arts and sciences.
He is mesmerized by
the insane celebration of lust and sexual passion.
He is mesmerized by
the insane celebration of lust and sexual passion.
Losing his dignity, losing his wisdom,
losing his dignity, losing his wisdom,
he is caught in the house of maya,
trapped by what he sees with his eyes and his mind.

After the dance is over,
he lies there, rolling on the ground, crying.
After his song is taken away,
his tongue flaps uselessly,
his eyes close, and
the sounds disappear from his ears;
he is just an actor helplessly
lying on the ground.

Thinking of this, he will cry
about all the acts he performed before,
about everything he decorated before.
"It was all for nothing!" he will shout.
"It was all false," he will say in retrospect.
"No one is helping me here," he will say.
"I have been deceived!" he will cry.
It is only then that he will say this.
"I have no one to help me!" he will say,
wailing in grief.
This is man's situation.
This is man's life.
Yet he lived without thinking of this.

Why didn't you think of this before, my *manamē?*
Why didn't you think of this before, my *manamē?*
Why didn't you think of this before?
Look, this is everyone's situation.
Look, this is everyone's situation.
Why did you allow yourself to be deceived by it too?

Look, the five and the six obligations are in your heart.
If you search for them with wisdom, *appa,*[1]
the six happinesses will come to you, and
you will understand the six tastes.
The six levels of wisdom will dawn.
The resonance "Allāhu" will descend.
His qualities, actions, and conduct will come into you.

As the Guru, as the Grace,
as the Guru, as the Grace, as your Father,
He will be there within you, teaching you.
One.
After that, you will lack nothing.
Know this.
Know this, my life.
*Āmīn.* May it be so.

---

1. *appa* (inter.) an interjection of happiness

# Help Us Know Prayer, O God

*Sunday, June 3, 1984, 9:00 A.M.*

PRAYING WITHOUT KNOWING the way,
praying without knowing any way at all —
this is what we do in the world when we pray.
We pray without knowing prayer.
Almighty One, we pray without knowing anything.

I do not know the prayers.
I do not know the formal prayers.
I do not know the prayers.
I do not know the formal prayers.
I do not understand the recitation or the reading.
I do not understand the recitation or the reading.

We flail about like lifeless corpses,
we wail without knowing *'ilm,* divine knowledge.
I do not know race, religion, or separation.
I am suffering.
O God, Almighty Indivisible Completion,
I simply believe that You are One.
I do not know race, religion, separation, or division.
I am confused.

I simply believe that You alone are my Master.
I simply praise You as the great Light of Ādi.

We are slaves, slaves;
rule over us, O God.
We are slaves, slaves;
rule over us, O God.
Help us know prayer.
Teach us how to recite and to read.
Show us the way to perform prayer and worship.

O God, open that truth.
O God, reveal the way to me and to my children,
to me and to my children.
O God, reveal the way to me and to my children.
Grant us the purity of heart
to pray to You with love, with certitude, and *īmān*
so we can worship one thing in unity,
so we can always live together as one family,
so we can embrace all lives with love and
gather them together as one.

Pour upon us the grace to embrace with faith
and to pray to God,
with the Light of grace, the divine luminous Light,
the Light of the pearl of *gnānam,*
with the Light of wisdom, the divine luminous Light,
the Light of the pearl of *gnānam.*
O great Light of Ādi,
embrace us and pour Your grace upon us.

Please pardon all the sins
we have committed unknowingly.
You, the God who rules the three worlds,
You Yourself must embrace us.
We are ignorant sinners.
You must embrace us and rule over us,
O God, Allāhu.
Pour Your compassion upon us,
open Your eyes, and
look at us.

Thoughts of earth and maya have come to mesmerize us.
The religions and separations have come to shake us,
to make us lose our dignity.
The races, religions, and separations have come to
catch us and squeeze us.
Each second they are hurting us.
What can we do?
They are hurting us.
What can we do, O God?

Help us to escape from them,
just as You escaped from them,
O Most Able One.
Protect us with Your grace, O God.
Protect us with Your grace, O God.
You are the one God
who is beyond the bounds of imagination.
Protect us with Your grace, O God.
Watch over us with Your grace.

O Treasure of the greatest bliss.
O Ruler,
O Qādir, O Powerful One,
O Dastagīr, O Lord,
O my Eye,
O my Gem,
O our Source of Light,
O God, O Indivisible Completion,
Allāhu,
end the suffering of the poor.
Protect each one of us.
End the suffering of the poor.
Protect each one of us.
Look at us, protect us.

O Treasure of the Greatest Bliss,
O Great Father, O God,
O Great Ruler,
Rabbil-'ālamīn, Lord of the Universes,
O Great Ruler,
Rabbil-'ālamīn, Lord of the Universes,
O Rahmān,
we need Your blessing.

Dwelling as the Life within life,
You must open the *qalb* of truth and
feed us with the honey which is grace,
to make blissful *'ilm*, wisdom, clarity, and *imān* grow,
to make the fruit of *gnānam* grow,
so we can partake of
the fruit of wisdom, the fruit of *gnānam*, the fruit of grace,

so we can partake of
the fruit of wisdom, the fruit of *gnānam*, the fruit of grace.
We must be given that taste!
O God, help me and my children.
O Blissful God, O God,
Yā Rabbil-ʿālamīn, O Lord of the universes.
*Āmīn. Āmīn. Āmīn. Āmīn.*
*As-salāmu ʿalaikum wa rahmatullāhi*
*wa barakātahu.*
May it be so. May it be so. May it be so. May it be so.
May the peace, the beneficence, and
the blessings of God be upon you.

# Glossary

The following traditional supplications in Arabic are used through-out the text:

⌣ *sallAllāhu 'alaihi wa sallam,* may the blessings and peace of Allāh be upon him, is used following the Prophet Muhammad, the Rasūlullāh, the Messenger of Allāh.

⌣ *'alaihis-salām,* peace be upon him, is used following the name of a prophet or an angel.

⌣ *radiyAllāhu 'anhu* or *'anhā,* may Allāh be pleased with him or her, is used following the name of a companion of the Prophet Muhammad ⌣, *qutbs,* wives of the prophets, and exalted saints.

Unless otherwise noted, the following words are Tamil, a Dravidian language whose origins in antiquity are unknown.

## Pronunciation Key

The non-Arabic and non-Tamil reader of this book will encounter strange words and names. We have tried to make them as simple as possible to pronounce.

While there are standard ways of transliterating Arabic letters into Roman script, there is no standard system of transliterating Tamil. Thus, we have not adopted any system in its entirety, but are indebted to many.

We have simplified the consonants—for the typical English speaking person, it would not be particularly helpful to distinguish between the two types of s or h or t in Arabic or the two types of t or the three types of n or l in Tamil.

gn is pronounced like the ng in king or like the ñ in the Spanish word mañana

k has been variously transliterated as k or j or g, depending on whether it has a hard, medium, or soft sound

th (a confusing and inconsistently applied legacy transliteration that has come down from the German) has been simplified throughout as t or d, depending on sound

We have adopted the phonetic spelling of words, such as *meecham* and *shari,* that have been incorporated into common usage in Philadelphia.

Both Arabic and Tamil have long and short vowels: the long vowels have been indicated by long marks in most cases. Thus, in Arabic and Tamil,

a is pronounced as in agree,

ā is pronounced as a long ā in father;[1]

i is pronounced as in pin,

ī is pronounced as a long ī as in pique;

u as in pull,

ū as a long ū in rule;

o is pronounced as in opaque,

ō is pronounced as a long ō in ore;

e is pronounced as in end,

---

1. In Arabic the long ā is generally pronounced with a flatter vowel sound, more like man than father, except after r and six emphatic consonants.

ē   is as a long ē in they;

ai   is pronounced as in aisle except at the end of a word, where it is generally pronounced as in day.[2]

Any good transliteration system, of course, needs to be logically consistent. However, the idiosyncrasies of both languages must be considered; a few well-placed exceptions serve to clarify a sound that would otherwise be mangled. For instance, *nāi* (dog—pronounced as in high) could not be spelled *nāy* without causing confusion, even though that is what the Tamil spelling would seem to indicate.

# A

*'abd* (Arabic n.) slave, servant

*adab* (Arabic n.) good manners, decency, humaneness, culture, courtesy, propriety, as exemplified in the life of Prophet Muhammad ⊕

Ādi, *ādi* (n.) God; the beginning, primal beginning, source, origin

Ādi Param (n.) God, the Most Great

Ādi Rahmān (Tamil & Arabic n.) God, the Most Compassionate

Ahamad (n.) [Lit. most praiseworthy] the beauty of the heart; the beauty of the heart brings about the beauty of the countenance, *muham*, of Muhammad ⊕. That beauty is the beauty of Allāh's qualities. This is a name that comes from within the ocean of divine knowledge, *bahrul-'ilm*. Allāh is the only One who is worthy of the praise of the heart.

*aiyō* (inter.) oh, oh no

*ākhirah* (Arabic n.) *Ākhirah* is where the soul proclaims the First *Kalimah* to Allāh. "There is nothing but You, O Allāh!" This is

---

2. However, in Arabic the *ai* is pronounced as the *ay* in day, except after r and six emphatic consonants when it is pronounced like the *ai* in aisle.

the ultimate and final realization, it is the soul's exclamation as it perceives who it is, and with this final realization and expression, the soul that is a ray of God's Light returns to the One Omnipresent God. The soul returns to the Source from which it came. There is only One—Allāh. Where all this happens is called *ākhirah*.

*'ālamul-arwāh* (Arabic phrase) the world of pure souls

*al-hamd* (Arabic phrase) The praise; the five letters, *alif, lām, mīm, hā',* and *dāl,* of the Arabic alphabet, which constitute the heart. They become transformed in the heart of a true human being into *al-hamd,* the praise of Allāh.

*al-hamdu, al-hamdu lillāh, al-hamdu lillāhi* (Arabic phrase) all praise is to Allāh

*alif* (Arabic n.) The first letter of the Arabic alphabet, equivalent to the English letter a and to the Arabic numeral 1. To the transformed man of wisdom, *alif* represents Allāh, the One who stands alone.

Allāh, Allāhu (Arabic n.) God

*allu* (v.) take

*āmīn* (Arabic n.) may it be so

*anādi* (n.) the beginningless beginning; the state of darkness before creation; the state in which God meditated upon Himself alone; the period of pre-creation when Allāh was alone and unmanifest, unaware of Himself even though everything was within Him; the state before *ādi*

*ānmā* (n.) soul, life

*appa* (inter.) an interjection of happiness

*as-salāmu 'alaikum wa rahmatullāhi wa barakātahu kulluhu* (Arabic phrase) May all the peace, the beneficence, and the blessings of God be upon you.

*a'ūdhu billāhi minash-shaitānir-rajīm* (Arabic phrase) I seek refuge in God from the accursed satan.

*awwal* (Arabic n.) [Lit. *al-awwal,* the first] the state in which forms begin to manifest

# B

*Bismillāhir-Rahmānir-Rahīm* (Arabic phrase) In the name of God, the Most Compassionate, the Most Merciful.

# C

Chennai (n.) [Lit. the city of Chennai in India, formerly Madras] Chennai symbolizes the liberation that results from the annihilation of the self.

# D

Dastagīr (Persian n.) Lord

*dhāt* (Arabic n.) the essence of God, His treasury, His wealth of purity, His grace

*dhikr* (Arabic n.) The remembrance of God. Of the many *dhikrs,* the most exalted *dhikr* is *"Lā ilāha illAllāhu:* There is nothing other than You. Only You are Allāh." All *dhikrs* relate to His *wilāyāt* or His actions, but this *dhikr* points to Him and to Him alone.

*dīn* (Arabic n.) [Lit. religion, faith, path] perfect purity, its Light and its truth; the resplendence of perfectly pure *imān,* absolute faith, certitude, and determination; the Light of truth for *dunyā,* the world, and *ākhirah,* the hereafter

*dunyā* (Arabic n.) the world

# E

*enna* (interjection) [Lit. what] Don't you agree?

# F

*faqīr* (Arabic n.) religious mendicant, ascetic, pauper

*fikr* (Arabic n.) contemplation, meditation, concentration on God

# G

Gnāna Guru (phrase) the divinely illumined teacher who has attained the state of grace-awakened wisdom; the guide who can lead the way to God

*gnānam* (n.) divine wisdom, grace-awakened wisdom

*gnāni* (n.) a wise man, a man of divine wisdom

Guru (n.) the Shaikh, the Teacher who awakens the truth within the disciple; the Guide who takes the disciple to the shore of the heart

# H

*hayāh* (Arabic n.) life

*hikmat* (Arabic n.) the secrets of wisdom

# I

*'ibādah* (Arabic n.) worship and service to God

*illAllāhu* (Arabic phrase) Only You are Allāh. You alone exist.

*'ilm* (Arabic n.) divine knowledge

*īmān* (Arabic n.) absolute and unshakable faith that God alone exists; the complete acceptance by the heart that God is One

*indira jālam* (phrase) the magic of maya which extends into space

*inmay* (n.) this life; the here

*insān* (Arabic n.) man, a human being

*Insān Kāmil* (Arabic n.) a perfected human being; one who has realized Allāh as his only wealth, cutting away the wealth of the world and the wealth sought by the mind; one who has acquired God's qualities, performs his own actions accordingly, and immerses himself within those qualities; one in whom everything other than Allāh has been extinguished

*kalimah* (Arabic n.) *Lā ilāha illAllāhu:* There is nothing other than You, O God. Only You are Allāh. The recitation or remembrance of God that cuts away the influence of the five elements of earth, fire, water, air and ether, washes away all the karma that has accumulated from the very beginning until now, dispels the darkness, beautifies the heart and causes it to resplend. The *kalimah* washes the body and the heart of man and makes them pure, makes his wisdom emerge and impels that wisdom to know the self and God.

karma (n.) The qualities of the connection to hell. There are two kinds of karma: inherited and acquired. Inherited karma is made of the qualities formed at the time of conception by the qualities in the minds of the parents. Inherited karma is dispelled when the Gnāna Shaikh accepts a disciple as one of his children. Acquired karma is formed as the result of our good and evil deeds. Acquired karma must be dispelled by the children themselves.

Khudā (Persian n.) God

# L

*lām* (Arabic n.) a letter in the Arabic alphabet, corresponding to the English consonant l, which stands, within the realm of wisdom, for the Nūr, Light, the Light of wisdom

# M

*mālay* (n.) garland of flowers, a string of pearls, religious beads

*manamē* (n.) heart, mind, self, life

*mānidan* (n.) Man, human being

*mantira jālam* (phrase) magic performed through the use of mantras

*marumay* (n.) the hereafter, the next realm

maya (n.) illusion

maya *jālam* (phrase) the magical performances of illusion

*mīm* (Arabic n.) a letter in the Arabic alphabet, corresponding to the English consonant m, which stands, within the realm of wisdom, for Muhammad ⊕

*mubārakāt* (Tamil & Arabic n.) blessings in the three worlds; *mu* (n.) is a Tamil prefix meaning three; *barakāt* (Arabic n.) means blessings

Muhammad ⊕ (Arabic n.) the beauty of the Light of Allāh's essence present in the heart and reflected in the face; Muhammad ⊕, the Messenger of God, the last of the line of prophets

*munivar* (n.) an ascetic

# N

Nabī ⊕ (Arabic n.) the Prophet Muhammad ⊕

*nafs, nafs ammārah* (Arabic n.) [Lit. person, spirit, personality, inclination, or desire which goads or incites one towards evil] the seven kinds of desires, that is, desires meant to satisfy one's own pleasure and need for comfort

Nūr (Arabic n.) Light; the resplendence of Allāh; the plenitude of the Light of Allāh that has the resplendence of a hundred million suns; the completeness of Allāh's qualities. When the plenitude of all these becomes One and resplends as One, that is His Light, His Nūr. That is Allāh.

Nūr Muhammad (Arabic n.) one of the nine aspects of Muhammad; the aspect that is wisdom

# P

Pādishah (Persian n.) King of Kings

*pahut arivu* (n.) Divine analytic wisdom; the sixth of the seven levels of wisdom. Muhaiyaddeen ☺. The wisdom of Allāh that explains His mysteries to the soul. This explanation is the Qur'ān.

*pillay* (n.) child

*purānas* (n.) the seventeen evil qualities within man [Lit. an ancient story, a legendary tale or myth]

# Q

Qādir (Arabic n.) God, the Powerful

*qalb* (Arabic n.) Heart, the heart within the heart of man, the inner heart. Bawa Muhaiyaddeen ☺ explains that there are two states for the *qalb*. One state is made up of four chambers, which represent Hinduism, Fire Worship, Christianity, and Islām. Inside these four chambers there is a flower, the *qalb-bū* that contains the beauty and fragrance of the divine qualities of Allāh. This is the second state, the flower of grace, *rahmah*.

*qalb-bū* (Arabic & Tamil phrase) the flower of the heart

Qudrah (Arabic n.) Power of God

Qur'ān (Arabic n.) The words of Allāh that were revealed to His Messenger, Prophet Muhammad ☺; those words that came from Allāh's Power are called the Qur'ān; Allāh's inner book of the heart; the Light of Allāh's grace which comes as a resonance from Allāh.

Qutb ☺ (Arabic n.) One who has attained the power of the Light of grace-awakened divine analytic wisdom that dawned from the throne of God and that investigates, understands, and analyzes everything in the eighteen thousand universes and beyond; through this inner analysis, the darkness of evil is dispelled and the beauty of goodness is made clear and radiant. Sent by Allāh through His grace and mercy, to reawaken mankind's faith in God and to establish certitude in our hearts, the Qutb ☺ is the wondrous embodiment and illustration of *imān*, absolute faith in God, in all three worlds.

# R

Rabb (Arabic n.) God, the Lord, the Creator

Rabbil-'ālamīn (Arabic n.) the Creator of the universes

*rahmah* (Arabic n.) compassion, grace, mercy

Rahmān (Arabic n.) God, the Most Compassionate; merciful

*rāni* (n.) queen

Rasūl ☺ (Arabic n.) Prophet Muhammad ☺, the Messenger of Allāh

*rasūl* (Arabic n.) a messenger of Allāh; a man of wisdom

*rūh* (Arabic n.) The soul, the Light ray of God, the Light of God's wisdom. Bawa Muhaiyaddeen ☺ explains that the *rūh* is life, *hayāh*. Out of the six kinds of lives, the soul is the Light life, the human life. It is a ray of the Nūr, the Light of Allāh, a ray that does not die or disappear. It comes from Allāh and returns to Allāh.

# S

*sabūr* (Arabic n.) [Lit. *sabūr* is the intensive form of *sabr* or patience] Patience; inner patience; to go within patience, to accept it, to think and reflect within it. *Sabūr* is that patience deep within patience which comforts, soothes, and alleviates the suffering caused by the mind.

*salām* (Arabic n.) greeting of peace

*salawāt* (Arabic n.): Prayers asking for blessings for the Prophet ☺, for the believers, and for everyone. *SallAllāhu 'alā Muhammad;*

*sallAllāhu 'alaihi wa sallam.* May Allāh bless Muhammad; May Allāh bless him and grant him eternal peace. *SallAllāhu 'ala Muhammad; ya Rabbi salli 'alaihi wa sallim.* May Allāh bless Muhammad; O my Lord. Bless him and grant him peace.

*sayyid* (Arabic n.) a title of respect for a descendant of Prophet Muhammad ⊕; leader, chieftain

*selvam* (n.) wealth

*selvom* (phrase) we will leave

Shaikh (Arabic n.) the Guru; the teacher who takes the disciples to the shore of the heart; a spiritual teacher

shaitān (Arabic n.) satan

*shari* (n.) all right

*shukūr* (Arabic n.) gratitude; contentment with whatever may happen, realizing that everything comes from Allāh; contentment arising from gratitude

*sūrah* (Arabic n.) chapter of the Qur'ān (when spelled with a *sīn);* form (when spelled with a *sād)*

*Sūrah* of *Al-hamd* (Arabic n.) The Chapter of Praise in the Qur'ān. Another name for the *Sūratul-Fātihah.*

*Sūratul-Fātihah* (Arabic n.) The opening chapter of the Qur'ān: Praise be to Allāh, the Cherisher and Sustainer of the Worlds; the Most Compassionate, the Most Merciful; Master of the Day of Judgment. Thee alone do we worship, and only Thine aid do we seek. Show us the Straight Way. The way of those on whom Thou has bestowed Thy Grace, those whose (portion) is not wrath, and who go not astray.

*Sūratul-Ikhlās:* (Arabic n.) The Chapter of Purity in the Qur'ān: He is Allāh, the One and Only; Allāh, the Eternal, the Absolute; He begetteth not, nor is He begotten; and there is none like unto Him.

swami (n.) teacher, ascetic

# T

*tambi* (n.) brother

*tangam* (n.) gold

*tangom* (phrase) we will go

*tārahan, singhan, sūran* (n.) the three sons of maya; the three aspects of the sex act

*tarittiram* (n.) troubles

*tarittirom* (phrase) we will not tarry

*tawakkul, tawakkul-'alAllāh, tawakkulun 'alAllāh* (Arabic n. & phrase) absolute trust in God; surrender to God; handing over to God the entire responsibility for everything

*toluhay* (n.) worship, prayer; most often refers to the formal five-times prayer in Islām

# U

*ummah* (Arabic n.) followers, people, community, nation

# W

*waqt* (Arabic n.) Time of prayer. In the religion of Islām, there are five specified *waqts,* times of prayer, each day. But truly, there is only one *waqt*—the prayer that never ends, wherein one is in direct communication with God and merged with God.

*wilāyah, wilāyāt* (pl.) (Arabic n.) God's Power; that which manifests through God's actions; the ninety-nine beautiful names and actions of God

# Y

Yālpānam (n.) Jaffna, a city in northern Sri Lanka

yā Rabbal-'ālamīn (Arabic phrase) O Creator of all the worlds

# Index

*Passim* denotes that the references are not to be found on all of the listed pages; e.g., 24-29 *passim* would be used where the reference is on pages 24, 25, 27, and 29.

# Books by
# M. R. Bawa Muhaiyaddeen ☺

Life Is a Dream: A Book of Sufi Verse

A Timeless Treasury of Sufi Quotations

The Four Virtues and Their Relationship
to Good Behavior and Bad Conduct

Bawa Asks Bawa Muhaiyaddeen ☺ (Volumes One & Two)

*Sūratur-Rahmah:* The form of Compassion

God's Psychology: A Sufi Explanation

The Point Where God and Man Meet

The Map of the Journey to God: Lessons from the School of Grace

The Golden Words of a Sufi Sheikh, Revised Edition

Islam and World Peace: Explanations of a Sufi, Second Edition

A Book of God's Love

The Resonance of Allah: Resplendent Explanations
Arising from the *Nūr, Allāh's* Wisdom of Grace

The Tree That Fell to the West: Autobiography of a Sufi

*Asmā'ul Husnā:* The 99 Beautiful Names of Allah

Questions of Life—Answers of Wisdom (Volumes One & Two)

The Fast of Ramadan: The Inner Heart Blossoms

*Hajj:* The Inner Pilgrimage

The Triple Flame: The Inner Secrets of Sufism

A Song of Muhammad ☺

To Die Before Death: The Sufi Way of Life

A Mystical Journey

Sheikh and Disciple

Why Can't I See the Angels: Children's Questions to a Sufi Saint

Treasures of the Heart: Sufi Stories for Young Children

*(continued on next page)*

Come to the Secret Garden: Sufi Tales of Wisdom

My Love You My Children: 101 Stories for Children of All Ages

*Maya Veeram* or The Forces of Illusion

God, His Prophets and His Children

Four Steps to Pure *Īmān*

The Wisdom of Man

Truth & Light: Brief Explanations

Songs of God's Grace

The Guidebook to the True Secret of the Heart (Volumes One & Two)

The Divine Luminous Wisdom That Dispels the Darkness

Wisdom of the Divine (Volumes One to Six)

The Tasty, Economical Cookbook (Volumes One & Two)

## Booklets
Gems of Wisdom series:

Vol. 1: The Value of Good Qualities

Vol. 2: Beyond Mind and Desire

Vol. 3: The Innermost Heart

Vol. 4: Come to Prayer

## Pamphlets

Advice to Prisoners

Come to Prayer: The Wake-up Song

*Du'ā' Kanzul-'Arsh* (The Invocation of the Treasure of the Throne)

Faith

The Golden Words of a Sufi Sheikh: Preface to the Book

The Instructions: The Fox and the Crocodile and Do Not Carry Tales

The Instructions: God Is Very Light

The Instructions: Unity

Islam & World Peace: Explanations of a Sufi –
*Jihād,* The Holy War Within

## A Contemporary Sufi Speaks:

*(continued on next page)*

## Foreign Language Publications

Ein Zeitgenössischer Sufi Spricht über Inneren Frieden
(A Contemporary Sufi Speaks on Peace of Mind—German translation)

Deux Discours tirés du Livre L'Islam et la Paix Mondiale:
Explications d'un Soufi
(Two Discourses from the Book, Islam and World Peace:
Explanations of a Sufi—French translation)

¿Quién es Dios? Una Explicatión por el Sheikh Sufi
(Who is God? An Explanation by the Sufi Sheikh—Spanish translation)

## Other Publications

Bawa Muhaiyaddeen Fellowship Calendar

Morning *Dhikr* at the Mosque of Shaikh M. R. Bawa Muhaiyaddeen ☺

For free catalog or book information call:
**(888) 786-1786 or (215) 879-8604 (voice mail)**

For information about books and pamphlets by M. R. Bawa
Muhaiyaddeen ☺ and CDs and DVDs of his discourses,
please visit **www.bmfstore.com**

For information about
Muhammad Raheem Bawa Muhaiyaddeen ☺,
the Bawa Muhaiyaddeen Fellowship,
the Mosque of Shaikh M. R. Bawa Muhaiyaddeen ☺,
and the *Mazār* of Shaikh M. R. Bawa Muhaiyaddeen ☺,
please visit **www.bmf.org**

# About
# M. R. Bawa Muhaiyaddeen ☺

The teachings of Muhammad Raheem Bawa Muhaiyaddeen ☺
express the mystical explanation, the SUFI path of esoteric
Islam; namely that the human being is uniquely created with
the faculty of Wisdom, enabling one to trace consciousness
back to its origin—Allah, the one divine Being, the Creator of
all—and to surrender the self within that Source, leaving the
One God, the Truth, as the only reality in one's life. He spoke
endlessly of this Truth through parables, discourses, songs and
stories, all pointing the way to return to God.

People from all religions and races flocked to hear and be
near him; he taught everyone, regardless of origin, with love,
compassion and acceptance. An extraordinary being, he taught
from experience, having traversed the Path, and returned,
divinely aware—sent back to exhort all who yearn for the
experience of God to discover this internal Wisdom, the path
of surrender to that One.

M. R. Bawa Muhaiyaddeen's known history begins in Sri
Lanka. He was discovered in the pilgrimage town of Kataragama
by spiritual seekers from the northern city of Jaffna. Begging
him to come teach them, he did so for forty years until 1971,
when he accepted an American invitation to Philadelphia, from
where he lovingly taught until his passing in December, 1986.

In these distressing times, his teachings are increasingly recognized as representing the original intention of Islam which is Purity—the relationship between man and God as explained by all the prophets of God, from Adam to Noah, Abraham, Moses, Jesus and Muhammad, may the peace of God be upon them—all sent to tell and retell mankind that there is one and only one God, and that this One is their source, attainable, and waiting for the return of each individual soul.

The Bawa Muhaiyaddeen Fellowship is in Philadelphia, Pennsylvania, which was the home of M. R. Bawa Muhaiyaddeen ☺ when he lived in the United States. The Fellowship continues to serve as a meeting house, as a reservoir of people and materials for everyone wishing access to his teachings.

The Mosque of Shaikh M. R. Bawa Muhaiyaddeen is located on the same property; here the five daily prayers and Friday congregational prayers are observed. An hour west of the Fellowship is the Mazār, the resting place of M. R. Bawa Muhaiyaddeen ☺ which is open daily between sunrise and sunset.

If you would like to visit the Fellowship, or to obtain a schedule of current events, branch locations and meetings, please contact:

Bawa Muhaiyaddeen Fellowship
5820 Overbrook Avenue
Philadelphia, Pennsylvania 19131

Phone: (215) 879-6300
Fax: (215) 879-6307

E-mail: **info@bmf.org**
Website: **www.bmf.org**

*Al-ḥamdu lillāh!*
All praise belongs to God!